Salads

Checkerboard Cookbooks

NEW YORK

Introduction

Salads—Flavor, Nutrition, and Eye Appeal

WHEN TO SERVE SALAD

In the first century A.D., the Roman poet Martial debated in verse whether it is best to serve salad at the beginning of a meal or after the first courses. Evidently, this minor but complicated culinary argument has been with us longer than most people would imagine. There is a sound case to be made for either side in this age-old dispute: that is to say, a cook should feel free to serve salad whenever he or she wishes, so long as the salad is appropriate to the foods preceding and following it.

It would seem sensible that a salad served before the entrée be at once interesting in itself —since it is, in effect, a first course—yet not so heavy or cloying as to destroy the diners' appetites for what is to come. At the beginning of a meal, for instance, an *antipasto*, that bountiful, random assortment of piquant, pungent, fairly salty foods (salami, prosciutto, cheese, olives, pickled vegetables, anchovies, etc.), will stimulate the appetite; it is often served with or followed by such raw vegetables as fennel, celery, lettuce, and radishes, intended to "refresh" the palate. An entirely vegetable salad, with such components as fresh mushrooms, sweet peppers, raw onion, or zucchini, could also be served first, especially if accompanied with plenty of good, coarse-grained bread. *Crudités*, a variable and colorful assortment of raw or very lightly steamed vegetables served with perhaps a choice of

dressings or dips, have become increasingly popular as first courses and buffet staples in a diet-conscious society. The fact that they may be prepared well in advance of a meal is also in their favor.

What salad—if any—to serve with a main course is more problematic, because it all depends on what the main course is. If it is a subtle, fairly complex dish (say, a delicately sauced fish, roast duck, or braised veal shoulder with sauce or stuffing), the salad should be something quite simple, no more than one or two kinds of greens tossed in a mild vinaigrette dressing. Also, it should probably be brought on as a separate course, just before fruit and cheese or a light dessert. If the salad is served with the main course, the crunchiness of the raw vegetables and the strong acid taste of vinegar or citrus juice in the dressing may distort or dampen the flavors both of other foods and of fine wines. But served afterward, perhaps with good-quality bread or bread sticks, the salad will refresh the palate and give diners a welcome pause to prepare for the subsequent courses.

As any true food-lover knows, on the other hand, there is great pleasure to be had in combining salads with certain hearty main courses. A particularly delicious meal might pair grilled or roasted meat or fowl with a tossed salad dressed with garlicky mustard vinaigrette. A potato, rice, or pasta salad would make such a meal even more substantial, if desired. The taste problem of mixing wine and vinegar on this sort of menu can be solved by serving a robust plain table wine, preferably red, or else hard cider or beer.

Sometimes salad *is* the meal. With a simple accompaniment of fresh crusty bread and butter in generous quantity, any of the fish, meat, and pasta or rice salads in this recipe book will make a delicious and labor-saving lunch or supper, particularly during the warmer seasons. When enjoying such an unpretentious feast, you might keep in mind that you are eating much the same wholesome fare which has nourished peoples around the world for many centuries.

SOME REMARKS ABOUT FRESH GREENS

Nearly all salads include greens, even if only as a garnish. To most Americans, "greens" means iceberg lettuce, and perhaps it strikes some people as finicky, even heretical, of food writers to continually lambast that old standby salad fixing. But iceberg did not, in fact, become so generally popular in this country until just a couple of decades ago, when supermarket suppliers discovered that this variety of lettuce traveled better and had longer shelf life than other greens. To this day, it remains virtually unknown throughout most of Western Europe and in much of the rest of the world. Its lack of popularity is well deserved. Although iceberg does pack a formidable crunch, it has very little savor relative to other greens, and its excessive wetness can dilute the flavor of other salad ingredients and dressings.

Even though iceberg lettuce has definitely become the most readily available and least expensive salad green in this country, if you shop around, you should be able to find at least some of the other greens mentioned in these recipes, and at a fairly reasonable price. Particularly easy to find are romaine lettuce (used in Caesar salads), Boston lettuce, and, in summer, when local produce becomes available at the supermarket, various kinds of leaf lettuce, which may range in color from pale green to

ruby red. Chicory, Belgian endive, and radicchio may not be stocked by your grocer if you live beyond a large metropolitan area, but even the dandelion greens that bedevil your own front lawn can supply an interesting, tasty change of pace. If you have never ventured out of iceberg territory before and are not sure how to identify alternative greens at the market, you might refer to the illustrations of various salad greens shown elsewhere in this Introduction. In addition, a generous glossary of salad greens is provided further on in the Introduction.

Even if you do decide to stick with iceberg as the mainstay of your saladmaking, there is no reason why you cannot make your salads more interesting by adding small amounts of other greens. In Roman times and the Middle Ages, people were fond of combining strongly contrasting and, by our standards, rather peculiar flavors in salads. One favorite Roman combination, for example, consisted of shredded meat (perhaps doormice!), fish oil, and bitter greens, while medieval cooks added mint, borage, fennel, and other highly aromatic, almost perfumy herbs to their salads, as well as three or four different kinds of onions. Some of this salad history remains deliciously vestigial in the habits of present-day cooks, who often add small handfuls of more pungent greens to simple lettuce salads. Commonly used are such bitter greens as Belgian endive, chicory, escarole, dandelion, and bitterest of all, the vivid reddish "green," radicchio. Arugula (or rocket), once commonly cultivated in America and recently rediscovered by salad chefs and gourmet cooks, imparts a peppery taste to salads. Watercress, crunchier and less juicy than arugula, lends similar tanginess. Sorrel, often sold as "sour grass," has a puckery flavor that reminds some people of lemons. While such greens are too strong-flavored to be eaten alone, when used imaginatively in combination with blander lettuces they add a delicious, subtle accent to the simplest tossed salads.

Varieties of Salad Greens

Endive

Italian Romaine

Arugula

Chicory

Radicchio

Escarole Heart

Romaine Lettuce

Bibb Lettuce

BUYING AND STORING FRESH GREENS

The enthusiasm that good cooks display toward food and eating is especially reflected in a quest for foods which are wholesome and fresh. In the best of worlds, it would be ideal to have your own vegetable patch, even a small kitchen garden, providing opportunities to mingle favorite homegrown salad vegetables with a variety of greens to make the freshest and tastiest of salads. More commonly, however, dependence on the local market is necessary. In warm seasons, market availability of locally grown produce supplies choices nearly as good as a home garden would. American modernization of large-scale agriculture and long-distance transport of produce has afforded us the good fortune to be able to find year-round in the supermarket many vegetables and salad greens available only seasonally in other countries. But these same ''advances'' are responsible for iceberg lettuce and for pink tomatoes that taste rather like unripe melons. It is indeed a bargain with the devil—but we can get the better of it by keeping our eyes open when shopping for produce.

Be choosy about the market where you buy your salad greens. Unless they enjoy a very brisk turnover in produce, a first-rate green-grocer will keep all greens in refrigerated bins and will stand some very fragile greens (watercress, arugula) in ice water. And be choosy about which greens you select. Avoid anything that looks wilted, soft, shriveled, rusty or otherwise discolored, or in some other, maybe indescribable way not quite right. To get the most for your money, especially when salad greens are sold by the piece rather than by the pound, pick greens that feel dense and heavy, not those which look large. An appealingly large head of Boston or romaine lettuce, escarole, or chicory may be composed of large, floppy outer leaves that will generally prove too tough and bitter to be used in a salad; it is the crisp, pale green, moisture-heavy inner leaves you want. Heads of iceberg lettuce are also remarkably varied with respect to weight and density; again, the denser heavier heads are always a better buy. One further note: When you are lucky enough to be able to purchase leaf lettuce grown by local truck farmers or gardeners, avoid plants that sport a long, thick central core from which the leaves sprout like spray from a fountain. Such plants have ''bolted'' due to unfortunate weather conditions, and are likely to be off-tasting.

On the subject of storing greens in the home refrigerator, a great deal of incomplete and sometimes contradictory advice has been written. One recommendation, for example, is to not wash salad greens prior to putting them in the refrigerator, but this admonition probably strikes most people as so odd that they wash the greens anyway. (Who wants a refrigerator full of pesticides and mud?) The rationale for not washing greens until serving time is that washing can bruise them, thus shortening their storage life; but if you are careful and wash the greens under a very gentle flow of water, you are not likely to damage them significantly.

Then there are all those do's and don't's about what sort of container to keep greens in. One practice widely favored of late is to store greens in open plastic bags. This does work. But with the possible exception of watercress, which cannot properly withstand being stored for longer than a day or so in any manner, greens are also very happily kept in a tightly sealed plastic container. (There are containers on the market shaped expressly to accommodate heads of lettuce.) And yes, though you are told by nearly everyone not to do it, greens can be detached from the clump or head—though preferably not torn in pieces—and then refrigerated for a day, or even two, without appreciable harm. For longer storage, it is best to leave greens untorn and intact.

PREPARING GREENS FOR SALAD

An unavoidable fact about salad greens, regardless of variety, is that they must be washed thoroughly before being eaten. The necessity of carefully rinsing the leaves can be obvious in cases where dirt or sand still adheres to the plant; but even when greens are apparently grit-free, the practice is recommended for washing away any invisible pesticide that may have been used in growing.

Although the process is admittedly a bit of a nuisance, greens must really be dried well before being used in a salad. Wet greens water down the salad dressing; in fact, the dressing can hardly stick to them at all. (Remember how reluctant oil and water are to mix.) And soggy greens destroy one of the pleasanter sensations of a good fresh salad—its satisfying crispness.

There are several methods of drying greens. Salad dryers are available in a variety of styles, beginning with the classic wire basket which is filled with greens and vigorously spun (outdoors), allowing centrifugal force to draw off excess water. An imported coated aluminum model is designed for use in a sink or basin. Salad ''spinners'' are not only available in such expensive metal forms; a type popular in the United States in recent years, made of plastic, has a spinning mechanism surrounded with an outer bowl to catch the water spun off the wet greens. Dryers generally have limited capacity, about enough to dry lettuce for only five or six servings of salad at one time. If you do not wish to invest in a salad spinner, you can dry greens quite acceptably by hand. Set intact leaves, curved side down, in a single layer either on a large cloth towel or on a double or triple thickness of paper toweling. Then gently pat dry—*don't rub*—the exposed surface of the leaves with more towels. If there is time, chill the greens for up to several hours in a salad bowl lined with paper or cloth towels (you may also intersperse paper towels among the greens), and the leaves will end up as dry as desirable.

Many cooks specify that greens be torn rather than cut before being put in a salad; but this practice is not sacrosanct. To some people, torn greens look more elegant than those which have been cut, and cut greens do have a tendency to turn brown along the cut edge if they stand a while before being served. But when lining a bowl with lettuce, it is often much easier to cut than to tear, especially if the leaves must have a certain shape in order to fit the contours of the salad bowl. Also, chiffonade strips of lettuce certainly have their place in salads, particularly if you are using iceberg, which has a more distinct taste when shredded than when it is torn apart in large chunks. But whether you cut or tear, remember one thing: except for Caesar salad, where half the fun is in picking up long, whole spears of romaine lettuce with your fingers, salad greens should be chopped or torn into pieces small enough to fit easily into the average human mouth. Few things are more awkward for a table guest than having to maneuver from plate to palate a large, floppy piece of lettuce dripping with salad dressing.

NOTES ON OTHER SALAD INGREDIENTS

Let's begin with that favorite salad ingredient—*tomatoes*. Though it may come as a surprise to some readers, many salad enthusiasts oppose adding tomatoes to tossed salads at all, claiming that tomatoes leak juice and thereby spoil the taste of the dressing. You can minimize this problem, however, by slicing the tomatoes lengthwise, rather than in rounds or wedges; for some reason, tomatoes sliced from top to bottom retain most of their seeds and juice. Local late-summer tomato crops provide flavor so much superior to the fare available at other times that many cooks recommend tomatoes be used in salads only then, as a seasonal treat.

Many recipes in this book call for *olives*. Ordinary bottled green olives, with or without pimento stuffing, available in any grocery store

9

will work fine in salads, though the larger, un-pitted Greek or Italian olives sold in delicatessens and specialty shops have a more briny, truer taste. When a recipe calls for black (or ripe) olives, avoid using the California ones packed with liquid in cans: these are most likely green olives which have been darkened chemically and are virtually flavorless. Instead, buy black olives that have been cured in salt and packed dry; these can be bought by weight or else in glass jars and are often imported. If these olives prove a bit too strong or salty for your taste, simmer them for a minute in water just to cover, then pat dry.

As for *cheeses*, American products generally tend to be blander than their imported counterparts. Our mozzarella, for instance, is made from cow's milk rather than the more flavorful milk of water buffaloes as is done in Italy. However, a bit of marinating in some olive oil, freshly ground pepper, and salt enlivens it nicely. Regular blue cheese makes a fine substitute for Gorgonzola, especially if you find a good brand made primarily from whole milk, one that looks well-veined with blue. As for Parmesan, what is sold in the round cardboard shakers cannot in the least be compared with the genuine item. Look instead for small, whole wedges of Parmesan at the supermarket, and grate the cheese yourself. (A food processor makes quick work of this task: simply cut the cheese in half-inch bits and process with the metal blade.) Wedges of Romano cheese are tasty, often more widely available substitutes for Parmesan in most recipes. When you're in the mood to indulge yourself, pick up a small piece of genuine imported Italian Parmesan at a specialty cheese shop—quite expensive, but since the flavor of good, freshly grated imported Parmesan is so pronounced, you may need only half as much as you usually use.

When it comes to using *herbs* in salads, a conservative hand can be the most successful. Neither French nor Italian cuisine is half so herb-oriented as many people think, and their use might more often consist of rubbing a wooden salad bowl with a sprig of fresh thyme or rosemary but seldom actually adding these herbs, either fresh or dried, to a salad or salad dressing. Basil and parsley, among the most commonly—and abundantly—used herbs in Italian salads, should always be added fresh, sometimes in large pieces (whole leaves of basil, small sprigs of parsley), sometimes chopped. Fresh basil can be found in specialty food markets throughout the summer, but if you don't have it on hand, you are better off substituting a few pinches of dried oregano in a recipe than using dried basil, which by comparison has little taste. Fresh parsley, available year-round at the supermarket, should never be replaced by so-called parsley flakes. The larger, flat-leaf variety and the smaller, crinkly-leaf variety are both flavorsome.

Vinegar has recently come into its own as a food product, and we now find a wide selection available. But as a shrewd old Italian proverb has it, "To make a fine salad it takes a big spender to pour the oil, but a miser for the vinegar." In other words, vinegar should be added sparingly or you may ruin the taste of the salad and set your guests to gasping uncomfortably. This is not to say, however, that vinegar is of no importance, for it is the bite from this ingredient which sets off the flavors of the salad fixings. For best flavor, choose a good-quality wine vinegar, either red or white, that has been diluted to an acidity of 5 percent or less. Vinegars that have been steeped with herbs (typically, tarragon, basil, or rosemary) can be an excellent addition to salad dressings, but must be used in moderation—no more than a teaspoon per quarter cup of oil—or else your salad will end up tasting like an herb sachet. Often these herb vinegars are made with white vinegars, distilled from grain, which otherwise have very little taste and are really, more or less, acetic acid diluted with water. Cider vinegar has a flavor not well suited to many salads. Lemon juice makes an excellent salad dressing substitute for vinegar, particularly for all-lettuce salads or cooked salads.

Last but not least is the *oil*, the critical ingredient of any salad dressing. Since the selection of oil gives the salad its overall flavor, it is essential that the oil be of good quality. For this reason, the preferred choice is olive oil, that special ingredient which gives various Medi-

terranean cuisines their unique character. Olive oils differ tremendously in taste, quality, and price. Because domestic cooking and salad oils are not subject to official labeling or grading controls, they can be something of a gamble; but imported oils are all strictly regulated and labeled according to quality. Those imported oils which have been pressed (often by hand in cold-stone presses) from the finest olives are labeled "Extra Virgin," while those made from olives of lesser quality are called simply "Virgin." The lowest grade of olive oil is "Pure," made from the pulp (and sometimes the pits) of olives left over from initial pressing of Extra Virgin or Virgin oil.

It is often held that the world's finest olive oils originate in the area around Lucca, Italy. But for use in salads, where the olive taste needs to be pronounced, some of these very fine (and very expensive) oils turn out to be too subtle in flavor. Besides fine Italian and French olive oils, good-quality salad and cooking oils are imported from several other Mediterranean lands, including Spain, Portugal and Greece. On the other hand, certain obscure bargain brands are quite likely to be thick, greenish, and unpleasantly strong, even odoriferous. All in all, perhaps the best way to choose an olive oil is to shop around and experiment, buying small containers of several different brands until you find one whose qualities you like.

Among other widely available, less expensive food oils used for saladmaking, peanut oil and sesame oil are perhaps the most distinctive-tasting. Experiment with these oils a bit to determine if their flavors are to your liking. The many blended "vegetable oils" or "salad oils" on the market tend to be rather nondescript and bland in taste, and will add very little to your salad fixings.

SOME USEFUL NOTES FOR SALAD PREPARATION

Acidulated Water:
Prepare acidulated water by adding 3 tablespoons of lemon juice or white wine vinegar to 4 cups of water.

Blanch:
To blanch (or parcook) vegetables, simmer them in lightly salted water to cover. Usually a preliminary step in vegetable cookery, blanching can serve to loosen the skins of vegetables. Blanched fresh vegetables such as broccoli and cauliflower are both colorful and delicious when served slightly chilled with a creamy vinaigrette sauce.

Bouquet Garni:
Mixed seasoning used in cooking or other food preparation, usually consisting of parsley, thyme, bay leaf, and peppercorns tied in a cheesecloth bag. For some dishes, garlic, clove, rosemary, tarragon, fennel, celery seed, or other seasonings may be added. The bouquet garni is removed from the pot and discarded prior to serving.

Celeriac (Celery root):
This knobby, hairy root vegetable has a taste suggestive of celery. Wash the vegetable well, peel thoroughly and deeply, and parboil thin slices or julienne strips for up to 10 minutes in lightly salted water to cover. For use in salads, celeriac should remain crisp-tender.

Cheese:
For recommendations on using domestic and imported cheeses in salad recipes, see page 10.

Cucumbers:
If available, choose smaller, pale-skinned varieties, which will have better flavor. Because most commercial cucumbers are coated with wax, they must be peeled before using.

Greens:
For descriptions of and recommendations on greens, see the Glossary of Salad Greens on page 13, as well as pages 5-9 of the Introduction.

Herbs:
Use fresh herbs whenever possible to produce generally superior taste results. To substitute dried herbs for fresh, use only about one-third the amount called for in a recipe specifying fresh herbs. Since dried herbs are fragile, they should be kept in metal or ceramic containers, away from light and heat, and should be replaced every six months or so, for they soon lose their savor. For further information on herbs, see page 10.

Julienne:
To prepare vegetables in julienne strips, cut matchstick rods 1/8 to 1/4 inch thick and 2 to 3 inches long. Julienne vegetables can also be made with a food processor.

Olive Oil:
For notes on the purchase and use of olive oil, see pages 10-11.

Olives:
Information about olives is given on pages 9-10.

Onions:
The milder-flavored Bermuda and red Italian onions are probably best for using raw in salads. Always buy firm, unblemished onions with short necks and dry, crackly skin. These varieties will keep best if refrigerated in an airtight bag.

Peppers:
To peel fresh sweet peppers, either spear them with a long-handled fork and rotate over a gas flame until their skins begin to char and loosen from the flesh, or place them under a hot broiler, turning two or three times, until their skins have blistered and can be scraped off. Before using, peppers should be cored by having stem, seeds, and inner membrane removed.

Pickled Mixed Vegetables:
Cured in vinegar and salt, pickled mixed vegetables are sold in glass jars of various sizes, often labeled "garden salad," or *giardiniera*.

Tomatoes:
For remarks on tomatoes, see page 9.

Vinegar:
Information about the various types of vinegar is provided on page 10.

GLOSSARY OF SALAD GREENS

Arugula (Rocket):
A peppery, smoky-tasting salad green, best used as a savory accent in combination with other greens.

Belgian Endive:
A small, cylindrical head lettuce with tightly packed, cream-colored leaves tapering to a point. Endive is comparatively expensive, but the smooth texture and slightly bitter flavor of one small head will greatly enliven a salad.

Bibb Lettuce (Limestone):
A small head lettuce with soft, subtly flavored, tongue-shaped leaves.

Boston Lettuce (Butterhead; Simpson):
Though its leaves are larger and floppier than those of Bibb lettuce, Boston lettuce is in other respects quite similar to Bibb and is more readily available in supermarkets.

Chicory (Curly Endive):
Long, spiked-leaf stalks form a large, bushy, elongated clump or head. The outer stalks are dark green and a bit tough, especially toward the base; the pale green inner stalks, more tender yet crisp, are most prized for salads. Chicory can be quite bitter, so many people like to combine it with blander greens in a salad.

Corn Salad (Lamb's lettuce; Field salad):
Tender, small-leaved greens that can be used alone for salads, or else in combination with other greens.

Dandelion Greens:
Dandelion greens have a tart, slightly bitter flavor. Those picked in spring, before the plant has blossomed, are milder-tasting and more tender than mature leaves.

Escarole:
Italian cuisine adds the large, dark green, scoop-shaped outer leaves to soups, or cooks them like spinach to serve as a vegetable course. The crisp, pale inner leaves, which have a taste similar to romaine lettuce, are often served in salads with a strongly flavored dressing.

Iceberg Lettuce:
The old standby, available everywhere in the U.S. but less flavorful than other greens. If you do use it, choose dense, heavy heads for the best results.

Leaf Lettuce:
There are many varieties of leaf lettuce. The leaves may be crinkly, curly, or scalloped, ranging in color from light green to dark red. All varieties are quite delicate in taste and texture. Handle gently when washing and drying.

Radicchio:
This small, ruby-red head lettuce rather resembles a miniature head of red cabbage. It is the bitterest of all salad greens and has a chewy texture. An expensive vegetable, radicchio is worth seeking out at specialty markets, for its tangy and distinctive flavor and lovely color make it a great addition to tossed salads.

Romaine Lettuce (Cos):
An elongated head lettuce with crisp, flavorful, spear-shaped leaves, romaine may either be torn and combined with other salad greens or left in whole leaves tossed with hearty dressings, grated cheese, or seasoned croutons.

Salad Bowl:
This Australian lettuce has long, thin leaves somewhat resembling oak leaves. Soft-textured and delicate in flavor, salad bowl can be served alone or mixed with other greens.

Sorrel (Sour grass):
Young and tender sorrel leaves, used sparingly, add a piquant, lemony flavor to salads.

Spinach:
Small, tender spinach leaves can be added whole to salads, combining especially well with such other ingredients as hard-cooked eggs and fresh mushrooms. A favorite dressing for spinach salads is bacon bits with blue cheese.

Watercress:
A classic garnish for grilled and roasted meats, watercress also makes a fine addition to tossed salads. In cleaning it, tough stalks should be trimmed off and discarded. Watercress should be used as soon as possible after purchase. For optimum storage for a day or two, stand tied bunches in an inch of water, cover loosely with plastic wrap, and refrigerate.

Basic Salad Dressings

Aioli (Blender)

Yield: about 1½ cups

3 large garlic cloves, chopped
1½ Tb lemon juice (or wine vinegar)
½ tsp salt
3 egg yolks
1 cup olive oil

In the blender container, place garlic, lemon juice, salt, and egg yolks. Cover and blend on high speed until smooth.

Uncover and add the oil in a slow, steady stream; then blend on low speed. When sauce is so thick that oil becomes hard to incorporate, add 1 or 2 tablespoons of water, then add remaining oil. (This dressing is an appropriate accompaniment for nearly all raw vegetable salads or makes a tasty dip for crudités.)

Blue Cheese Dressing

Yield: about ⅔ cup

2 Tb Gorgonzola (or other blue cheese)
salt
1 Tb lemon juice
black pepper, freshly ground
5 Tb olive oil

Mash cheese in a small mixing bowl. Add salt to taste, lemon juice, a pinch of fresh ground pepper, and mix well. Gradually pour in oil, beating steadily with a fork to blend well. (This dressing is best suited for a variety of raw vegetable salads.)

Egg Dressing

Yield: about ⅔ cup

1 hard-cooked egg
salt
black pepper, freshly ground
2 Tb wine vinegar
oregano (optional)
6 Tb olive oil

In a small bowl, mash egg yolk with a fork. Season to taste with salt and fresh ground pepper; add vinegar, and mix well. (A pinch of oregano may be stirred in for additional flavor.) Gradually pour in oil, beating steadily to blend well. After salad ingredients have been tossed with the dressing, egg white can be chopped or grated as a garnish for the salad. (This dressing is suitable for nearly all raw salads.)

Garlic Dressing

Yield: about ½ cup

1 garlic clove
2 Tb wine vinegar
salt
black pepper, freshly ground
6 Tb olive oil

Mash garlic through a press into a small mixing bowl. Add vinegar and salt and fresh ground pepper to taste, beating with a fork until salt dissolves. Gradually pour in oil, and continue beating until well blended. (This dressing is particularly suited for leafy green salads and potato salad.)

Herb Dressing

Yield: about ½ cup

salt
black pepper, freshly ground
2 Tb wine vinegar
6 Tb olive oil
1 Tb minced basil, parsley, chives, or tarragon
  (or any combination)

In a small mixing bowl, beat salt and fresh ground pepper together with vinegar until salt dissolves. Gradually pour in olive oil, and blend well. Stir in minced herbs, let stand briefly to absorb flavor, and then stir well again before pouring over salad. (This dressing is well suited for a variety of raw and cooked salads.)

Horseradish Dressing

Yield: about 1 cup

salt
3 Tb wine vinegar
½ cup oil
black pepper, freshly ground
1 hard-cooked egg
1–2 Tb grated horseradish

Dissolve a pinch of salt in vinegar, beat in oil with a fork, and season lightly with fresh ground pepper. Press egg yolk through a sieve into dressing, add horseradish to taste, and blend well. Egg white can be cut in julienne strips and used as garnish for serving salad.

Lemon Dressing

Yield: about ½ cup

alt
lack pepper, freshly ground
Tb lemon juice
Tb olive oil

In a small mixing bowl, combine a generous pinch of salt and fresh ground pepper with lemon juice. Beat well with a fork until salt dissolves. Gradually pour in oil, while continuing to beat to blend thoroughly. (This dressing is particularly suited to cooked salads.)

Mayonnaise

Yield: about 2 cups

egg yolks (at room temperature)
½ tsp salt
½ tsp dry mustard
¼ cup olive oil
¼ cup vegetable oil
Tb lemon juice (or wine vinegar)

Beat egg yolks together with salt and mustard until thick and lemon-colored. Combine olive and vegetable oils, and add drop by drop to the yolk mixture, beating constantly. As mixture thickens, oil may be added a little faster. Stir in lemon juice and blend well, then chill.

Mayonnaise Variations

Curry Mayonnaise:

To 1 cup of basic mayonnaise recipe, add about ½ tsp of curry powder, and blend well.

Green Mayonnaise:

To 1 cup of basic mayonnaise recipe, add bout ¼ cup of puréed watercress, spinach, r parsley (or some combination of these reens), and blend well. (This dressing goes ery well with egg salads.)

Herb Mayonnaise:

To 1 cup of basic mayonnaise recipe, add to 3 tablespoons of minced tarragon, parsley, or basil, and blend well.

Piquant Mayonnaise:

To 1 cup of basic mayonnaise recipe, add a dash of cayenne pepper and/or paprika, and blend well.

Sweet Cream Mayonnaise:

To 1 cup of basic mayonnaise recipe, add ¼ cup of heavy cream, and blend well. (This dressing is excellent for fruit salads and some raw vegetable combinations.)

Mayonnaise (Blender)

Yield: about 1¼ cups

1 egg
½ tsp dry mustard
½ tsp salt
2 Tb lemon juice (or wine vinegar)
½ cup olive oil
½ cup vegetable oil

In the blender container, place the egg, mustard, salt, and lemon juice.

Combine olive and vegetable oils, and pour ¼ cup of oil mixture into blender. Cover and turn on low speed. Uncover immediately, and pour in remaining oil in a steady stream. Blend until smooth and thickened, then chill.

Mustard Dressing

Yield: about ½ cup

1 tsp dry mustard
salt
2 Tb wine vinegar
6 Tb olive oil
black pepper, freshly ground (optional)

In a small mixing bowl, combine mustard, a pinch of salt, and vinegar, then beat with a fork until salt dissolves. Gradually pour in olive oil, and mix well. A pinch of fresh ground pepper can be added if tangier flavor is desired. (This dressing is particularly suited to salads made with raw or cooked vegetables.)

Creamy Mustard Dressing

Yield: about 1 cup

1 hard-cooked egg
1 tsp Dijon mustard (or grated horseradish)
2 Tb wine vinegar
salt
black pepper, freshly ground
¾ cup heavy cream

In a small bowl, mash egg yolk with a fork. Add mustard (or horseradish), vinegar, and salt and fresh ground pepper to taste, and mix well. Gradually pour in heavy cream, and blend thoroughly. After salad ingredients have been tossed with the dressing, egg white can be chopped or grated and used as a garnish for the salad. (This dressing is well suited to salads made with cold meats, cheese, or shellfish, as well as various raw vegetables.)

Avocado and Celery Salad (p. 21)

Orange Dressing

Yield: about ¾ cup

2 Tb fresh orange juice
1 tsp lemon juice
salt
black pepper, freshly ground
¼ apple, peeled and grated
pinch of dry mustard
5 Tb olive oil

Combine orange juice and lemon juice, and season with salt and fresh ground black pepper. Beat with a fork until salt dissolves. Stir in grated apple, mustard, and oil, blending thoroughly. (This dressing is particularly suited to fruit salads.)

Parmesan Dressing

Yield: about 1 cup

1 egg
½ cup olive oil
3 Tb wine vinegar
salt
black pepper, freshly ground
3–4 Tb grated Parmesan cheese

To coddle the egg: Place in a small pot of cold water, bring quickly to a boil, reduce heat, and simmer for exactly 1 minute. Plunge egg immediately into cold water.

In either a jar with a tight cover or a blender, combine oil, vinegar, coddled egg, salt and fresh ground black pepper to taste, and grated Parmesan. Mix thoroughly, and use immediately. (This dressing is especially good with mixed leafy green salads, possibly garnished with diced Bel Paese or some other semisoft cheese.)

Vinaigrette Dressing

Yield: about ½ cup

salt
black pepper, freshly ground
2 Tb wine vinegar
6 Tb olive oil

Combine a generous pinch of salt and fresh ground pepper with vinegar in a small mixing bowl, and beat well with a fork until salt dissolves. Gradually pour in oil, and continue beating until thoroughly blended. (This dressing can be used on a great variety of salads, particularly those made with leafy greens and other raw or cooked vegetables.)

Fresh Salads

Avocado and Celery Salad

Yield: 4 servings

lettuce leaves
4 center stalks celery, cut in strips
2 ripe avocados, peeled and cut in chunks
⅓ cup almond halves
2 hard-cooked eggs, cut in thin wedges
salt and pepper
2 Tb wine vinegar
4 Tb oil
2 Tb heavy cream
1 tsp grated horseradish
½ tsp chili sauce

Set a bed of lettuce leaves on each of four salad plates. Arrange celery strips and avocado cubes on them; garnish with almonds, and surround with egg wedges.

Blend a pinch each of salt and pepper with vinegar and oil. Add heavy cream, horseradish, and chili sauce. Beat thoroughly with a fork to blend well, taste for seasoning, and pour dressing over salad mixture.

Avocado and Cucumber Salad

Yield: 4 servings

2 cucumbers
salt
1 head lettuce
small tender spinach leaves (optional)
2 avocados
black pepper, freshly ground
juice of ½ lemon
½ cup oil

Peel and dice cucumbers, salt lightly, and set aside. Wash and dry lettuce leaves well, and line a salad bowl with them. Wash and dry spinach. Peel and dice avocados. Dry cucumbers well, toss gently with spinach and diced avocado, and spread mixture on bed of lettuce leaves.

Combine a pinch of salt and fresh ground pepper, lemon juice, and oil, and blend well. Pour dressing over salad, and toss lightly before serving.

Blue Cheese Dressing (see Index) would also go well with this salad.

Avocado and Lettuce Salad

Yield: 4 servings

1 large head lettuce
several sprigs of watercress
1 medium-cooked egg*
1 tsp dry mustard
4 Tb lemon juice
½ cup oil
salt
black pepper, freshly ground
1 avocado

Rinse lettuce and watercress well, and trim stems from watercress. Dry thoroughly, and tear the greens into a salad bowl.

Peel egg, break open carefully, spoon yolk into a cup or small bowl. Combine yolk with mustard, 2 tablespoons of lemon juice, oil, salt and pepper to taste, and mix well with a wooden spoon. Mince or grate egg white, and blend into the dressing. Pour dressing over greens, and toss gently. Peel avocado and slice thin, dipping slices in remaining 2 tablespoons of lemon juice. Arrange avocado slices on top of greens, sprinkle generously with fresh ground pepper, and serve.

* Egg should be simmered gently for exactly 4 minutes, then plunged in cold water before peeling.

Piquant Cabbage Slaw

Yield: 4 servings

1 small cabbage (preferably Savoy)
½ tsp prepared mustard
½ cup milk
½ cup mayonnaise
salt
2 hard-cooked eggs, sliced

Wash and dry cabbage, and scoop out the heart and core to form a large shell. Chop cabbage heart fine, and place in a mixing bowl. Combine mustard, milk, mayonnaise, and salt to taste. Pour dressing over chopped cabbage, and toss thoroughly. Spoon the mixture into cabbage shell, and surround the filling with egg slices.

Raw Cabbage Salad with Mint

Yield: 4 servings

1 garlic clove, cut in half
½ small, firm cabbage
3–4 celery stalks, chopped
juice of ½ lemon
salt and pepper
1 Tb fresh chopped mint*
5 Tb oil

Rub inside of a large wooden salad bowl with cut garlic clove. Shred cabbage, place in salad bowl, and add chopped celery.

In a cup or small bowl, combine lemon juice, salt, pepper, chopped mint, and oil; beat well with a fork. Pour dressing over cabbage mixture, and toss to coat well.

* If fresh mint is not available, a teaspoonful of sesame, fennel, or celery seeds would add interesting flavor and texture instead. If mint is not used, Creamy Mustard or Parmesan Dressing (see Index) would also go well with the basic ingredients of this salad.

Zucchini with Mixed Herbs (p. 70)

Gourmet Salad (p. 33)

Caesar Salad

Yield: 4 servings

½ cup olive oil
2 garlic cloves, cut in half
4 slices day-old bread, cubed
2 eggs
1 head romaine lettuce
4–6 anchovy fillets
1 tsp Worcestershire sauce
½ tsp dry mustard
2–3 Tb lemon juice
salt and pepper
⅓ cup Parmesan cheese

Heat half the oil, and sauté garlic until golden. Discard garlic, and sauté bread cubes in flavored oil, stirring gently until golden brown on all sides. Drain and set aside.

To coddle the eggs: Place in a pan of cold water, bring quickly to a boil, then lower heat and simmer for exactly 1 minute. Plunge eggs immediately into cold water.

Tear lettuce into bite-size pieces, and place in a salad bowl. In another smaller bowl, mash anchovies with a fork, and add remaining olive oil, Worcestershire sauce, mustard, and lemon juice; stir to blend well. Add salt and pepper to taste, mixing well and pour over lettuce. Break coddled eggs into a bowl, beat vigorously, and pour over the salad, tossing to coat well. Sprinkle with Parmesan cheese and croutons, toss gently but thoroughly, and serve immediately.

California Salad

Yield: 4 servings

2 oranges, peeled and sliced
2 cucumbers, peeled and sliced crosswise
1 grapefruit, peeled and segmented
1 large sweet pepper (red or yellow)
4 sweet gherkins, sliced in rounds or spears
several sprigs fresh parsley, chopped
salt
2 Tb white wine vinegar
½ cup oil
black pepper, freshly ground

Arrange orange slices in the center of a round platter. Make a circle of cucumber slices around the rim of the platter. (Note: After peeling grapefruit, discard all white pith and membrane.) Arrange grapefruit wedges between orange and cucumber slices.

Trim and rinse pepper, removing seeds and membrane; cut in thin strips, and scatter over orange slices. Garnish with sweet pickles and chopped parsley.

Dissolve a generous pinch of salt in vinegar, add oil, and mix well. Season lightly with fresh ground pepper, and pour dressing over salad.

Cantaloupe Boats with Yogurt Dressing

Yield: 4 servings

2 firm ripe cantaloupes
¼ lb Swiss cheese, diced
1 cucumber, diced
salt and pepper
1 cup plain yogurt
2 Tb mayonnaise
1 tsp lemon juice
2 hard-cooked eggs, cut in wedges
lettuce leaves

Slice melons in half, remove seeds and membrane, and carefully cut out most of the pulp, without piercing the skin and leaving a firm shell. Dice melon pulp, combine with cheese and cucumber, season lightly with salt and pepper, then stir gently to blend. Fill melon shells with the mixture.

Blend yogurt, mayonnaise, and lemon juice; mound the creamy dressing over the centers of the melon boats. Garnish each with egg wedges. On a serving platter, make a bed of lettuce leaves, and set melon boats on top to serve.

Carrot and Gorgonzola Salad

Yield: 4 servings

1½ lb carrots
½ cup Gorgonzola (or other blue cheese)
1 cup heavy cream
2 Tb oil
salt
1 tsp cumin seeds

Peel and rinse carrots; cut them in paper-thin slices. Press Gorgonzola through a sieve into salad bowl. Stir in cream, oil, and salt to taste, then blend well. Toss carrot slices with dressing, and sprinkle with cumin seeds.

Shredded Carrots with Yogurt Dressing

Yield: 4 servings

1½ lb carrots
½ cup mayonnaise (see Index)
lemon juice
Worcestershire sauce
black pepper, freshly ground
salt
1 cup plain yogurt

Peel and rinse carrots; grate them on the coarse side of a grater, or shred in a food processor. Blend mayonnaise well with a few added drops of lemon juice, a dash of Worcestershire, and a pinch of fresh ground black pepper. Toss shredded carrots with mayonnaise, then season to taste with salt. Top with yogurt and serve.

Celery and Mushroom Salad

Yield: 4 servings

¾ lb fresh mushrooms
½ lb celery hearts
¼ lb Gruyère cheese, diced
¼ cup oil
juice of ½ lemon
¼ cup heavy cream
1 Tb brandy (or dry sherry; optional)
salt
black pepper, freshly ground

Separate mushroom caps and stems, re serving stems for other use. Slice mushroom caps and celery hearts paper-thin, place i a glass salad bowl, and add diced Gruyère In a cup or small bowl, combine oil, lemor juice, heavy cream and brandy; season to taste with salt and fresh ground black pepper, and blend well. Pour dressing over salad, and toss gently to coat.

Celery Salad with Truffle

Yield: 4 servings

1 celeriac (celery root), sliced thin
salt
juice of ½ lemon
½ cup oil
black pepper, freshly ground
1 celery heart, sliced thin
1 small head lettuce
1 small white truffle (or 3–4 large fresh mushroom caps)

Prepare celery root according to instructions given in the Introduction. In a cup or small bowl, dissolve a pinch of salt in lemon juice, add 2 tablespoons of oil and a pinch of fresh ground black pepper, and stir well. Put celery root and sliced celery heart in a salad bowl, pour on dressing, and toss to coat well. Let stand for about 1 hour for flavoring.

Drain celery, then return it to bowl and add lettuce leaves torn into bite-size pieces and remaining oil. Toss gently to coat. Grate or slice truffle very thin over salad to serve. (If mushroom caps are used, they should be sliced quite thin, and half of them added to the salad mixture and tossed gently. The remaining mushroom slices should be used as a garnish.)

Celery Sticks with Prosciutto Dip

Yield: 4 servings

2–3 slices prosciutto (or smoked ham), chopped
½ cup oil
1 tsp Dijon mustard
salt and pepper
1 tsp wine vinegar
2 celery hearts

Sauté chopped prosciutto in 2 tablespoons of oil, then transfer to a mixing bowl. Add remaining oil, mustard, a pinch of salt and pepper, and vinegar, blending well. Rinse celery, and dry thoroughly. Remove any stringy fibers with a vegetable peeler, then cut celery in sticks. Place ham dip in a small dish at the center of a serving platter, and surround with celery sticks to serve.

Crudités with Seasoned Oil (p. 29)

Cheese and Almond Salad

Yield: 4 servings

1 head lettuce
1 small bunch arugula (or dandelion greens; optional)
salt
2 Tb wine vinegar
½ cup oil
black pepper, freshly ground
¼ lb Swiss cheese (or Gruyère), sliced thin
½ cup sliced almonds

Rinse lettuce and greens, and dry thoroughly. Tear the leaves in pieces into a salad bowl. Dissolve a generous pinch of salt in vinegar, add oil and a pinch of fresh ground pepper, then mix well. Cut cheese in thin strips, and sprinkle over salad greens. Garnish with sliced almonds, pour on dressing and toss gently.

Cheese and Walnut Salad

Yield: 4 servings

1 small head romaine lettuce
1 bunch celery hearts, julienne
¾ cup shelled walnuts, chopped coarse
¼ lb Gruyère (or other semisoft cheese)
2 oz sharp Gorgonzola (or other blue cheese)
½ cup oil
salt and pepper
2 hard-cooked eggs, sliced

Rinse lettuce, dry thoroughly, and tear the leaves in pieces into a salad bowl. Add celery strips and chopped walnuts. Dice Gruyère, and add to the salad bowl; crumble the Gorgonzola and sprinkle on top. Pour oil over very slowly, and season to taste with salt and pepper. Toss gently, and garnish with egg slices to serve.

Cold Meat and Truffle Salad

Yield: 4 servings

1 celeriac (celery root)
1 butterhead lettuce
1 thick slice cooked ham, julienne
1 thick slice spiced tongue, julienne
salt
juice of ½ lemon
½ cup oil
1 small white truffle

Peel celeriac, slice paper-thin, and drop slices in cold acidulated water. Wash, dry, and shred lettuce, and put in a salad bowl. Add prosciutto and tongue strips to the lettuce.

Dissolve a pinch of salt in lemon juice, add oil, and mix well. Dry celeriac thoroughly, and combine with salad mixture. Pour on dressing, and toss gently to coat. Slice truffle paper-thin, and garnish salad with the slices.

Crudités with Seasoned Oil

Yield: 4 servings

1 celery heart
2 small heads fennel
1 bunch radishes
2 scallions (including green tops)
2 small tender artichokes*
2 medium-size (or 4 small) carrots
Juice of ½ lemon
8 Tb oil
Salt
Black pepper, freshly ground

Trim and rinse celery, fennel, radishes, and scallions, and dry well. Peel celery stalks of their stringy fibers if necessary, and cut fennel in wedges. Soak artichokes briefly in a bowl of acidulated water, dry thoroughly, and quarter them lengthwise. Trim, scrape, and rinse carrots well; cut in slender sticks. Arrange vegetables in a wide shallow dish or on a serving platter. Put 2 tablespoons of oil in each of four very small bowls, season with salt and fresh ground pepper, and serve one to each guest as a dip for the raw vegetables.

*If very tender young artichokes are not available, substitute some other raw vegetables such as cauliflower or broccoli flowerets, or sweet pepper strips.

Stuffed Cucumbers

Yield: 4 servings

4 large cucumbers
Salt
4 hard-cooked eggs
5 anchovy fillets, chopped
1 small onion, chopped
1 Tb prepared mustard
Black pepper, freshly ground
Oil
Horseradish, freshly grated (or 4 tsp prepared horseradish)

Trim ends off cucumbers, peel, and slice in half lengthwise. Scoop out seeds and some pulp from each to make little "boats." Blanch by plunging cucumbers in lightly salted boiling water for a few minutes. Drain and dry.

Press egg yolks through a sieve into a mixing bowl. Add anchovy fillets and onion, and season with mustard and a pinch of fresh ground pepper. Add just enough oil to make a thick paste, and fill cucumbers with the mixture. Top each cucumber boat with some grated horseradish (or about ½ tsp prepared), and serve lightly chilled. Chopped egg whites can be used as an additional garnish, if desired.

29

Dandelion Greens with Bacon

Yield: 4 servings

4–6 cups dandelion greens, coarsely shredded
2 scallions, chopped (including green tops)
4 slices bacon, cut in ½-inch strips
3 Tb cider vinegar
1 tsp sugar
¼ tsp dry mustard
salt
black pepper, freshly ground

Combine greens and chopped scallion in a salad bowl. Sauté bacon until crisp, then add vinegar, sugar, and mustard to the pan. Stir with a wooden spoon over low heat until sugar and mustard are dissolved and mixture is smooth. Add salt and fresh ground black pepper to taste, and blend well. Pour hot dressing over dandelion greens, toss thoroughly, and serve immediately.

Sliced Egg and Orange Salad

Yield: 4 servings

1 head chicory (about ½ lb)*
2 hard-cooked eggs, sliced
1 unpeeled orange, sliced thin
salt and pepper
½ cup oil
4 Tb fresh grapefruit juice
1 Tb mixed tarragon, chives, and parsley, chopped

Rinse chicory, trim off tough outer leaves, and dry thoroughly. Chop chicory fine, and place in a salad bowl. Spread egg and orange slices over the chicory. In a cup or small bowl, combine a pinch of salt and pepper, oil, and fresh grapefruit juice, blending well. Pour dressing over greens, and toss gently to coat. Garnish with mixed chopped herbs.

*A mixture of other greens, such as arugula, escarole, and a bit of tender sorrel can be added to, or substituted for, chicory.

Endive, Apple, and Walnut Salad

Yield: 4 servings

4 heads endive
½ cup shelled walnuts, chopped coarse
1 apple (Golden Delicious or other firm sweet variety)
juice of ½ lemon
salt and pepper
½ cup oil

Rinse and dry endive well, cut in bite-size pieces, and put in a salad bowl. Sprinkle walnuts over endive.

Peel, core, and dice apple, and place in a small bowl. Pour lemon juice over apple, toss to coat, then add to salad bowl. Season to taste with salt and pepper, pour in oil, and toss to mix thoroughly.

Blue Cheese Dressing (see Index) would also go well with this salad.

Country Salad (p. 56)

Fava Bean Salad

Yield: 4 servings

2 cups fresh fava (or lima) beans, shelled
½ lb Romano cheese, diced
½ cup olive oil
salt
black pepper, freshly ground

Remove and discard delicate skin of beans. Combine beans and diced cheese in a salad bowl. In a cup or small bowl, combine oil, salt, and a generous sprinkling of fresh ground pepper, then blend well. Pour dressing over beans and cheese, and toss gently to coat. Taste for seasoning, and add more salt and/or pepper if preferred

Sweet and Sour Fruit Salad

Yield: 4 servings

2 small melons
2 apples, diced
2 bananas, sliced
juice of 2 lemons
6–8 shelled walnuts, chopped
¼ cup oil
2 Tb heavy cream
pinch of paprika
1 tsp prepared mustard
salt and pepper
green leaf lettuce
4 walnut meats for garnish (or crushed pineapple;
   optional)

Cut melons in half, and remove seeds thoroughly. Scoop out pulp with a melon baller, taking care to leave shells intact. In a mixing bowl, place melon balls, diced apples, and banana slices, then sprinkle with 2 tablespoons of lemon juice. Add chopped nut meats, and toss gently.

In a cup or small bowl, combine oil, remaining lemon juice, heavy cream, paprika, mustard, and a pinch of salt and pepper, stirring well. Pour dressing over fruit and nuts, mix well, and spoon the mixture equally into melon shells. Wash and dry leaf lettuce well, and spread leaves on a large serving platter. Set 4 filled melon shells on the bed of lettuce to serve. You may also garnish each shell with a whole walnut meat or crushed pineapple.

Tangy Fruit Salad

Yield: 4 servings

1 large grapefruit
2 oranges
4 fresh figs, sliced
4 cooked artichoke hearts, quartered
lettuce leaves
¼ cup heavy cream
juice of ½ lemon
hot pepper sauce
2–3 slices fresh pineapple, cut in chunks (optional)
6–8 shelled walnuts (or pecans), chopped coarse
   (optional)

Peel grapefruit and oranges, carefully removing pith and white membrane, then break fruit into segments. Make a bed of lettuce leaves on a serving platter. Arrange grapefruit and orange segments, sliced figs, and artichoke wedges atop the leaves.

Combine heavy cream, lemon juice, and a drop of hot pepper sauce, blending thoroughly. Pour creamy dressing over fruit salad mixture to serve. You may garnish the salad with chunks of fresh pineapple and chopped walnut meats.

Gourmet Salad

Yield: 4 servings

lettuce leaves
a few leaves of radicchio (or heart of escarole; optional)
1 large cooked beet (about ½ lb)
1 celeriac (celery root)
¼ lb boiled ham, in 1 slice
¼ lb spiced tongue, cut thick
1 egg yolk
½ cup oil
salt and pepper
2 Tb catsup
¼ cup heavy cream

Wash lettuce and other salad greens, dry thoroughly, and line a salad bowl with them. Peel beet and celeriac (see Introduction), and cut into julienne. Trim all fat from ham, and cut both ham and tongue in julienne strips.

Place egg yolk in a mixing bowl, and gradually add oil in a thin stream, beating constantly with a fork. When sauce has attained consistency of thin mayonnaise, stir in salt and pepper to taste, catsup, and cream, then pour into a sauceboat.

Combine beet, celeriac, ham, and tongue strips; arrange atop greens in salad bowl, and serve with sauce on the side.

Greek Salad

Yield: 4 to 6 servings

1 medium-size head crisp lettuce, shredded
4 medium-size firm ripe tomatoes, cut in wedges
1 sweet green pepper, sliced in thin rings
1 red onion, sliced in thin rings
1 cucumber, sliced thin
6 radishes, sliced thin
½ cup olive oil
2–3 Tb red wine vinegar
1 tsp oregano
salt
black pepper, freshly ground
¼ to ½ lb feta cheese
10–12 black olives, pitted
fresh parsley sprigs

Combine vegetables in a large salad bowl. In a smaller bowl, mix oil, vinegar, and oregano, and season to taste with salt and fresh ground black pepper. Crumble in feta cheese, and stir well to blend. Pour dressing over the salad, and toss gently to coat. Garnish with olives and parsley sprigs, and serve immediately.

Grapefruit Boats

Yield: 4 servings

4 grapefruit
2 cucumbers, peeled and diced
1 cup plain yogurt
½ cup mayonnaise (see Index)
salt
black pepper, freshly ground
mint leaves (optional)

Cut a slice off the top of each grapefruit, and carefully scoop out the pulp; do not break through the skin. Discard pith, dice the fruit, and toss gently with cucumbers. Blend yogurt and mayonnaise; season with salt and fresh ground black pepper. Pour dressing over grapefruit and cucumbers, and toss gently to blend. Fill grapefruit shells with the mixture, and chill slightly before serving. (Grapefruit boats may be garnished with fresh mint leaves to serve.)

Harlequin Salad

Yield: 4 servings

2 firm ripe pears
¼ lb fontina cheese (in 1 piece), diced
1 pimento, cut in strips
6–8 shelled walnuts, chopped coarse
8–12 pitted black olives, sliced
1 head lettuce
salt
juice of ½ lemon
6 Tb oil
black pepper, freshly ground

Peel, core, and dice pears. In a large salad bowl, combine diced pears with cheese cubes, pimento strips, chopped walnuts, and olive slices. Rinse and dry lettuce well, then tear in pieces; add to salad mixture, and toss gently.

Dissolve a generous pinch of salt in lemon juice, and blend well with oil and fresh ground pepper. Pour dressing over salad, and toss gently to coat thoroughly.

Lettuce Salad with Aniseed

Yield: 4 servings

1 head romaine lettuce
2 Tb Gorgonzola (or other blue cheese)
½ cup oil
2 Tb lemon juice
salt
1 heaping tsp aniseed

Rinse and dry lettuce thoroughly; tear in bite-size pieces into a salad bowl. In a cup or small bowl, mash orgonzola with a fork, and combine with enough oil and the lemon juice to produce a thick creamy mixture. Then add remaining oil and salt to taste, pour over lettuce, and toss to coat well. Sprinkle aniseed over salad, and serve.

Summertime Stuffed Tomatoes (p. 77)

Tomato and Egg Salad with Herb Dressing (p. 45)

Creamy Lettuce Salad

Yield: 4 servings

2 heads Bibb lettuce (or Boston lettuce hearts)
2 oz mild Gorgonzola (or other blue cheese)
5 Tb heavy cream
2–3 Tb oil
2 Tb lemon juice
1 tsp chopped chervil
salt
2 slices toasted dark bread, cut in croutons

Wash and dry lettuce well. Separate into leaves, and place in a salad bowl. With a fork, mash cheese in a mixing bowl; then add heavy cream, oil, lemon juice, chervil, and salt to taste. Stir to blend well. Pour dressing over salad mixture, and toss to coat. Garnish with croutons to serve.

Lettuce and Watercress Salad

Yield: 4 servings

1 head Boston (or romaine) lettuce
1 bunch watercress
2 garlic cloves
fresh basil, minced
fresh mint, minced
oil
white wine vinegar
pinch of dry mustard
salt and pepper

Trim and rinse salad greens well. Dry thoroughly, tear in bite-size pieces, and place in a salad bowl. Cut garlic in very thin slices. In a smaller bowl or cup, combine basil, mint, and garlic with about 3 parts oil and 1 part vinegar. Add mustard powder, season to taste with salt and pepper, and blend thoroughly. Pour dressing over greens, and toss gently to coat.

Lettuce Heart Salad

Yield: 4 servings

4 small lettuce hearts (or small heads of Boston lettuce)
2 hard-cooked eggs, chopped
1 Tb chopped chives
pinch of tarragon
1 Tb wine vinegar
1 tsp Dijon mustard
⅓ cup oil
salt

Place each lettuce heart on a separate salad plate. In a small bowl, combine chopped eggs, chives, and tarragon, and mix gently. Open the lettuce hearts somewhat, and fill each center with a quarter of the egg mixture. Combine vinegar, mustard, oil, and a pinch of salt, and blend well. Pour dressing over stuffed lettuce hearts just before serving.

Stuffed Lettuce Heart

1 large head lettuce   *Yield: 4 servings*
½ cup oil
2 Tb wine vinegar
salt
2 carrots, julienne
2 sweet peppers, julienne
2 Tb milk
¾ cup ricotta cheese
pepper
celery salt
fresh parsley sprigs

Discard outer leaves of lettuce, and open up the heart to make a sort of basket. Combine oil, vinegar, and salt, and toss with julienne carrots and sweet peppers. In a small bowl, stir milk into ricotta, then season to taste with salt, pepper, and celery salt. Fill lettuce heart with the vegetable mixture, mound seasoned ricotta atop it, and garnish with a few sprigs of fresh parsley. When ready to serve, cut into wedge-shaped quarters at table.

Mexican Salad

Yield: 4 servings

10-oz pkg frozen artichoke hearts
1 head endive
1 small celeriac (celery root)
5 Tb oil
2 Tb wine vinegar
¼ cup mixed pickled vegetables, chopped
hot pepper flakes
sugar
salt
1 cooked beet, diced
1 hard-cooked egg, chopped

Cook artichoke hearts according to package directions until fork-tender but still firm. Let stand to cool, then slice lengthwise in quarters. Rinse endive, dry thoroughly, and slice thin. Peel celeriac, slice thin, and put slices in acidulated water to keep from discoloring. (Afterward, dry thoroughly before adding to salad.)

Combine oil, vinegar, chopped pickled vegetables, and a pinch each of hot pepper flakes, sugar, and salt, mixing well. In a salad bowl, combine artichoke wedges, sliced endive and celeriac, and diced beet. Pour dressing over vegetables, and toss gently. Garnish with chopped egg to serve.

Mixed Green Salad with Red Onions

Yield: 4 servings

1 small head lettuce (preferably butterhead)
1 small head chicory
1 bunch watercress
1 sweet pepper, cut in thin strips
1 large red onion
1 heaping Tb capers
5 Tb oil
salt and pepper
juice of 1 lemon

Rinse and dry lettuce, chicory, and watercress thoroughly. Tear lettuce and chicory into bite-size pieces, and put them in a salad bowl. Trim watercress, and add to bowl along with pepper strips. Slice onion rather thick, separate into rings, and add to bowl along with ½ tablespoon of whole capers. Chop remaining capers, and combine with oil, salt and pepper to taste, and lemon juice, stirring to blend well. Just before serving, pour dressing over salad, and toss gently to coat.

Mixed Salad with Creamy Mustard Dressing

Yield: 4 servings

1 sweet pepper (red or yellow), sliced thin
¼ lb Swiss cheese, diced
8–12 pitted green olives
1 tsp Dijon mustard
½ cup heavy cream
1 medium-size head lettuce
½ cup oil
2 Tb wine vinegar
salt and pepper
1 heaping Tb capers

Place sliced sweet peppers, diced cheese, and olives in a bowl. Combine mustard with cream, blend well, and pour over salad mix. Let stand to flavor well for about 1 hour, stirring from time to time.

Tear lettuce leaves into a salad bowl. In a cup or smaller bowl, beat together oil, vinegar, salt, and pepper. Pour dressing over lettuce, and toss to coat. Add reserved ingredients in mustard dressing, toss gently, and garnish with capers to serve.

Mixed Salad with Yogurt Dressing

Yield: 4 servings

4 medium-size cucumbers, diced
2 firm ripe tomatoes, sliced
2 carrots, julienne
1 small head endive
1 cup plain yogurt
4 scallions (including green tops), chopped
1 Tb chopped fresh parsley
1 tsp lemon juice
salt
black pepper, freshly ground
1 Tb red caviar (optional)

Place diced cucumbers, tomato slices, carrots, and endive (cut into bite-size pieces) in a salad bowl. In a cup or small bowl, combine yogurt, chopped scallions and parsley, lemon juice, a pinch of salt, and a generous sprinkling of fresh ground black pepper, and blend thoroughly. Pour dressing over salad mixture, toss to coat, and garnish with caviar to serve.

Mixed Vegetables in Cheese Cones

Yield: 4 servings

4 carrots, grated coarse
3 stalks celery, chopped
¾ cup mixed pickled vegetables, chopped*
1 cup mayonnaise (see Index)
8 slices fontina (or other semisoft cheese)
lettuce leaves for garnish
4–5 small white onions, sliced
fresh parsley sprigs

Wash and trim fresh vegetables. Combine carrots, celery, pickled vegetables, mayonnaise. Twist slices of fontina into cones, circled with a wide onion ring (or fastened with toothpicks), and fill with vegetable mixture. Arrange cones on a serving platter, and garnish with lettuce leaves, onion rings, and parsley sprigs.

*Mixed pickled vegetables are sold in jars as *giardiniera*, or "garden salad."

Cauliflower Salad (p. 53)

Mixed Vegetable and Cheese Salad

Yield: 4 servings

2 cucumbers
4 large lettuce leaves
2 tomatoes, sliced
1 bunch radishes, sliced
1 cup diced semisoft cheeses*
1 cup plain yogurt
½ cup mayonnaise (see Index)
juice of ½ lemon
salt and pepper
1 Tb chopped fresh chives

Peel and dice cucumbers, then put them in a bowl of water with some ice cubes. Refrigerate for at least 30 minutes; drain and dry. Put 1 large lettuce leaf (or several smaller ones) on each of four salad plates, and garnish with tomato and radish slices; sprinkle diced cucumbers and cheeses on top.

Combine yogurt, mayonnaise, lemon juice, and salt and pepper to taste; blend well. Pour a quarter of the dressing over each portion, and sprinkle with chopped chives. Chill slightly before serving.

*This may be a combination of Gruyère, Bel Paese, mozzarella, and sharp Muenster, or any other semisoft cheeses of your choice.

Pineapple Salad

Yield: 4 servings

1 head lettuce
½ ripe pineapple, trimmed and diced (or 1 medium-size can of diced pineapple)
1 8-oz container cottage cheese
½ cup oil
juice of 1 lemon
pinch of oregano
salt
black pepper, freshly ground
1 bunch radishes, sliced thin
8 anchovy fillets

Rinse and dry lettuce well. Line a salad bowl mostly with tender leaves from the heart. In another bowl, shred the remaining leaves, add diced pineapple, and mix with cottage cheese.

In a cup or small bowl, combine oil, lemon juice, and a pinch each of oregano, salt, and fresh ground pepper, blending well. Pour dressing over pineapple, cottage cheese, and lettuce mixture; stir gently, and spoon out on bed of lettuce leaves. Garnish with radish slices and crisscrossed anchovy fillets to serve.

Prune and Pineapple Salad

Yield: 4 servings

½ lb prunes
4 slices fresh ripe pineapple (or canned), diced
1 celery heart, sliced thin
juice of 1 lemon
1 tsp prepared mustard
5 Tb oil
salt
1 lettuce heart (or leaf lettuce)
2 tsp chopped parsley

Blanch prunes in boiling water for a few minutes. Remove pits, slice prunes, and place in a salad bowl. Add diced pineapple and sliced celery. In a cup or small bowl, combine lemon juice, mustard, oil, and a pinch of salt, blending thoroughly. Pour dressing over salad mixture, and toss gently to coat.

Make a bed of lettuce leaves on 4 salad plates, divide salad equally among them, and sprinkle each with ½ teaspoon of chopped parsley to serve. Orange Dressing (see Index) would also go well with this salad.

Rainbow Salad

Yield: 4 servings

1 small red onion
1 head lettuce
1 head chicory
1 carrot
1 sweet red pepper
1 sweet yellow (or green) pepper
10–12 stuffed green olives
1 firm ripe tomato, sliced
2 cucumbers, sliced thin
2 anchovy fillets
½ cup oil
2 Tb wine vinegar
salt
black pepper, freshly ground

Slice onion thin, and chill in a bowl of cold water for at least 1 hour. Rinse lettuce and chicory, dry thoroughly, and cut in thin strips. Cut carrot and sweet peppers in thin strips, and slice olives. Dry onion rings thoroughly, and place in a salad bowl with lettuce, chicory, tomatoes, cucumbers, carrots, peppers, and olives. In a cup or small bowl, mash anchovies with a fork, then add oil, vinegar, salt, and fresh ground pepper, stirring until smooth and well blended. Pour dressing over salad mixture, and toss gently to coat well.

Salad Marianne

Yield: 4 servings

½ lb tender young spinach
juice of ½ lemon
5 Tb oil
1 Tb Dijon mustard
1 Tb wine vinegar
salt
black pepper, freshly ground
2 apples, peeled and diced
12–16 black olives, pitted
2 hard-cooked eggs, sliced

Clean and trim spinach according to directions given in the Introduction; drain and dry thoroughly. Place in a salad bowl, and toss with lemon juice and 2 tablespoons of oil. Let stand for about 1 hour.

In a cup or small bowl, blend mustard with vinegar, remaining 3 tablespoons of oil, and a pinch of salt and fresh ground pepper. Add diced apples and olives to salad bowl, pour on mustard dressing, and toss. Garnish with egg slices to serve.

Salad Musetta

Yield: 4 servings

6 shelled walnuts, chopped coarse
salt and pepper
2 Tb wine vinegar
1 tsp Dijon mustard
½ cup oil
1 head red leaf lettuce
2 carrots, julienne (or shredded)
2 hard-cooked eggs

In a mixing bowl, combine chopped walnuts, salt and pepper to taste, vinegar, mustard, and oil; stir to blend well. Rinse lettuce, dry thoroughly, and tear leaves in bite-size pieces. Toss with half the dressing; toss julienne carrots with remaining dressing. Place lettuce in the center of a salad bowl, and spread carrots around the rim. Rice or press egg white through a sieve, then sprinkle over carrots. Rice egg yolks, and sprinkle over the lettuce. Toss again gently at the table just before serving.

Sailor's Salad

Yield: 4 servings

1 head Romaine lettuce
8–10 green (or black) olives, pitted
4 anchovy fillets, chopped
2–3 large scallions (including green tops), sliced
3½-oz can chunk tuna, drained
salt
2 Tb wine vinegar
6 Tb oil
black pepper, freshly ground

Rinse lettuce, dry thoroughly, and break into broad strips. Combine in a salad bowl with olives, anchovies, and scallions. Flake tuna with a fork, and add to the salad bowl. In a cup or small bowl, dissolve salt in vinegar, add oil, season to taste with fresh ground pepper, and beat with a fork to blend well. Pour dressing over salad, and toss gently to coat.

Sardine and Celery Salad

Yield: 4 servings

4½-oz can sardines
juice of 1 lemon
1 cup mayonnaise (see Index)
black pepper, freshly ground
½ cup milk
1 celery heart

Drain sardines, and press through a food mill or blend to a coarse purée in a food processor. Combine sardine purée with lemon juice and mayonnaise. Season generously with fresh ground black pepper, add milk, and blend thoroughly.

Trim and wash celery, dry thoroughly, slice thin, and place in a salad bowl. Toss well with half the sardine dressing, then cover with remaining dressing to serve.

Shepherd's Salad

Yield: 4 to 6 servings

4–6 cups torn mixed salad greens (e.g., lettuce, arugula, endive, spinach)
2 navel oranges, sliced thin
1 small red onion, cut in rings
½ cup diced Bel Paese cheese
6–8 pitted black olives, chopped (optional)
1 garlic clove, peeled
1 cup oil
⅓ cup lemon juice
pinch of sugar
salt
black pepper, freshly ground

In a large salad bowl, combine greens, orange slices, onion rings, cheese cubes, and chopped olives. In a smaller bowl or cup, combine garlic (crushed through a press), oil, lemon juice, sugar, salt, and a very generous sprinkling of fresh ground pepper. Beat vigorously with a fork until sugar and salt are dissolved. Pour dressing over salad, then toss gently to coat.

Tangy Meat Salad (p. 60)

Spinach Salad Mimosa

Yield: 4 servings

1 lb tender young spinach
1 tsp dry mustard
salt
juice of 1 lemon
½ cup oil
black pepper, freshly ground
2 hard-cooked eggs
2–3 scallions (without green tops), chopped

Clean and trim spinach according to directions given in the Introduction. Drain and dry thoroughly, then place in a salad bowl. In a cup or small bowl, dissolve dry mustard and a pinch of salt in lemon juice; add oil, and beat with a fork to blend well. Pour dressing over spinach, and toss to coat. Let stand for about 30 minutes for flavoring.

When ready to serve, sprinkle spinach salad generously with fresh ground pepper and toss lightly. Then, either rice egg yolks or press them through a sieve over the center of the bowl, making a single heap. Around this, rice the egg whites (or sprinkle chopped egg whites) in a ring, and garnish with chopped scallions to serve.

Sweet Pepper Salad with Anchovies

Yield: 4 servings

2 medium-size sweet peppers (preferably green or yellow)
2 hard-cooked eggs
2 firm ripe tomatoes, cut in wedges
8–12 pitted green olives
5 Tb oil
1 Tb chopped basil
4 anchovy fillets, chopped.
salt
black pepper, freshly ground

Wash and trim peppers, removing seeds and membrane, pat dry, and cut in thin strips. Peel and cut eggs in quarters lengthwise, and combine with pepper strips, tomato wedges, and olives in a salad bowl.

In a cup or small bowl, combine oil, basil, anchovies, a pinch of salt, and a generous sprinkling of fresh ground black pepper, stirring well. Pour dressing over salad mixture, toss thoroughly, and serve.

Tomatoes with Green Sauce

Yield: 4 servings

4 firm ripe tomatoes
salt
2 anchovy fillets
½ cup oil
2 Tb wine vinegar
2 Tb capers
3 Tb chopped basil
3 Tb chopped fresh parsley
2 hard-cooked eggs

Cut tomatoes in half crosswise, gently squeeze out seeds and loose pulp, and make large hollows in each tomato. Salt shells lightly, and invert on a rack or paper towels to drain for a few minutes. In a small bowl, mash anchovies with a fork; combine oil, vinegar, capers, and chopped basil and parsley, blending well. Pour equal amounts of green sauce into each tomato shell. Press eggs through a sieve directly onto tomato halves (or chop very fine and sprinkle on) to garnish for serving.

Savory Tomatoes with Herbs

Yield: 4 servings

4 large firm tomatoes
salt
black pepper, freshly ground
2 Tb chopped fresh basil
oregano
about 4 Tb olive oil

Cut tomatoes in half crosswise. Squeeze halves gently to eliminate seeds and some pulp. Season each with salt, fresh ground pepper, chopped basil, and a generous pinch of oregano. Pour 1 teaspoon or more of olive oil over each tomato half and serve.

Spicy Tomato Salad

Yield: 4 servings

4 firm ripe tomatoes, sliced
1 onion, sliced thin
1 celery stalk, cut in thin spears
1 tsp cumin seeds
2 anchovy fillets, chopped
salt
2 Tb wine vinegar
1 tsp prepared mustard
black pepper, freshly ground
½ cup oil
2 hard-cooked eggs, sliced

Place tomato slices in a salad bowl, sprinkle with sliced onion and celery, about ¾ teaspoon of cumin seeds, and chopped anchovy fillets.

In a cup or small bowl, dissolve salt in vinegar. Add mustard, fresh ground pepper, and oil, blending thoroughly with a fork. Pour dressing over salad mixture, and toss gently to coat. Garnish with egg slices, and sprinkle with remaining ¼ teaspoon of cumin seeds to serve.

Tomato and Egg Salad with Herb Dressing

Yield: 4 servings

1 garlic clove, cut in half
2 Tb herb vinegar
salt
black pepper, freshly ground
pinch of paprika
pinch of dry mustard
½ cup oil
4 ripe medium-size tomatoes, cut in wedges
4 hard-cooked eggs, quartered lengthwise
1 Tb chopped fresh basil (or 1 tsp dried)

Rub inside of shallow wooden salad bowl with cut garlic clove. In a cup or small bowl, combine vinegar, salt, and fresh ground pepper, beating with a fork until salt is dissolved. Add paprika, mustard, and oil, and blend well.

Place tomato and egg wedges in salad bowl. Sprinkle the dressing evenly over tomatoes and eggs, and toss gently to coat. Garnish with fresh basil to serve. (If using dried basil, add directly to the dressing and mix; an equal amount of dried oregano could also be substituted.)

Tomato and Mozzarella Salad

Yield: 4 servings

4 firm ripe tomatoes
½–¾ lb mozzarella cheese, dried
4 anchovy fillets, chopped
1 Tb chopped fresh basil
½ cup oil
salt
black pepper, freshly ground
12–16 pitted black olives

Slice tomatoes, and arrange them overlapping on a platter. Sprinkle diced mozzarella and chopped anchovies and basil evenly over the tomato slices. In a cup or small bowl, combine oil, salt, and fresh ground pepper, and blend well. Pour dressing over salad mixture, and garnish with olives. Garlic Dressing (see Index) would also go well with this salad.

Tomato and Pepper Rounds with Spicy Lemon Dressing

Yield: 4 servings

3 firm ripe tomatoes, sliced
2 sweet peppers (yellow or green), sliced in rings
salt
1 Tb lemon juice
1 Tb Dijon mustard
1 tsp grated lemon peel
1 garlic clove, chopped
1 tsp cumin seeds
1 tsp fennel seeds
½ cup oil
coriander leaves (optional)

Arrange tomato and pepper slices on a serving platter. In a small bowl, dissolve salt in lemon juice. Add mustard, grated lemon peel, chopped garlic, cumin and fennel seeds, and oil. Blend thoroughly, and sprinkle dressing lightly over sliced vegetables. This salad may be garnished with fresh coriander leaves to serve.

Spicy Tongue Salad

Yield: 4 servings

4 thick slices spiced tongue, diced
1 celery heart, sliced
¼ lb Gruyère (or Swiss) cheese, diced
1 hard-cooked egg
2 tsp prepared mustard
1 cup oil
juice of 1 lemon
salt and pepper
1 heaping Tb chopped sweet gherkins

In a salad bowl, combine tongue, celery, and cheese. Mash egg yolk in a mixing bowl, add mustard, and blend until smooth. Pour in the oil very gradually, beating constantly with a fork or whisk. When all the oil has been incorporated, add lemon juice and salt and pepper to taste, blending well. Stir in chopped gherkins, and then pour dressing over salad mixture; toss to coat well. Press egg white through a sieve or food mill directly on salad as a garnish before serving.

Spicy Tomato Salad (p. 45)

Tomato and Mozzarella Salad (p. 46)

Tuna and Tomato Fantasy

Yield: 4 servings

4 firm ripe tomatoes
salt
6½-oz can tuna, drained
1 celery heart, cut in strips
small jar mushrooms packed in oil, sliced thin
juice of ½ lemon
3 Tb oil
2 hard-cooked eggs
1 tsp chopped fresh parsley
½ cup mayonnaise
8 black olives, pitted

Cut tomatoes in half crosswise, gently squeeze out seeds and loose pulp, and make large hollows in each tomato. Salt shells lightly, and invert on a rack or paper towels to drain for a few minutes. Flake the tuna in a mixing bowl, and add celery, mushrooms, lemon juice, and oil; stir to blend well. Fill tomato shells with tuna mixture.

Chop egg whites and mash yolks separately, then mix yolks with chopped parsley. Spoon 1 tablespoon of mayonnaise over tuna stuffing at the center of each tomato shell. Garnish half of each shell with chopped egg white, and the other half with the egg yolk and parsley mixture. Place an olive atop each stuffed shell to serve.

Turkish Cucumber Dip

Yield: 4 or more servings

2 cucumbers
1 lb container plain yogurt (or sour cream)
1 small onion, minced
1 garlic clove, minced
2 Tb olive oil
1½ Tb finely chopped fresh dill (or 2 tsp dill weed)
salt
black pepper, freshly ground

Peel and dice cucumbers very fine. Place in a mixing bowl, and stir in yogurt. Add minced onion and garlic, olive oil, dill, a pinch of salt, and a generous sprinkling of fresh ground pepper, blending thoroughly. (Serve with triangles of pita bread or other crusty bread to use for dipping.)

Two-Cheese Salad

Yield: 4 servings

1 head lettuce
¼ lb Swiss cheese, julienne
1 Tb blue cheese
1 tsp Worcestershire sauce
1 Tb wine vinegar
salt
½ cup oil

Rinse and dry lettuce leaves thoroughly. Place in salad bowl, and cover with strips of Swiss cheese. Combine blue cheese, Worcestershire sauce, vinegar, a pinch of salt, and oil, then blend well. Pour dressing over salad, and toss gently before serving.

Watercress, Egg, and Cheese Salad

Yield: 4 servings

1 bunch watercress
½ lb Swiss cheese, diced
4 hard-cooked eggs, quartered
12–16 green olives, pitted
8 anchovy fillets
1 sweet green pepper, julienne
salt
juice of 1 lemon
½ cup oil
black pepper, freshly ground
⅓ cup grated Parmesan (or Romano) cheese

Trim stems from watercress, rinse, and dry thoroughly. Make a bed of watercress sprigs on a serving platter. Mound diced cheese in the center, and surround with a sunburst of egg wedges interspersed with olives. Garnish with anchovy fillets and sweet pepper strips.

In a cup or small bowl, dissolve a pinch of salt in lemon juice, add oil and fresh ground pepper to taste, and beat with a fork until well blended. Pour dressing evenly over salad platter, and sprinkle with grated Parmesan to serve.

Watercress, Endive, and Grapefruit Salad

Yield: 4 servings

1 bunch watercress
1 head endive
1 large (or 2 small) grapefruit
2 scallions (without green tops)
salt
2 Tb lemon juice
½ cup oil

Rinse well and trim stems from watercress. Wash, trim, and slice endive. Peel grapefruit, discarding all white pith and membrane, and separate into segments. Reserve a few segments for garnish and cut remaining grapefruit in chunks. Slice scallions thin, separate into rings, and soak rings in ice water for 10 minutes.

Put watercress, endive, and grapefruit chunks in a glass bowl. In a cup or small bowl, dissolve salt in lemon juice, stir in oil, and blend well. Pour dressing over salad mixture, and toss to coat. Garnish with reserved grapefruit wedges. Drain and dry scallions thoroughly, then sprinkle over salad.

Zucchini Salad

Yield: 4 servings

8 small zucchini
salt
2 Tb lemon juice
black pepper, freshly ground
⅓ cup oil
1 tsp chopped fresh mint

Put zucchini in a bowl of water with a few ice cubes, and refrigerate for about 2 hours. Drain and dry zucchini, trim off ends, and slice. In a cup or small bowl, dissolve a pinch of salt in lemon juice, then add a generous sprinkle of fresh ground black pepper, oil, and chopped mint. Beat with a fork to blend well, and toss chilled zucchini slices with dressing just before serving.

Cooked and Combination Salads

Artichoke, Potato, and Asparagus Salad

Yield: 4 servings

2 artichokes, boiled
1 lb new potatoes, boiled and sliced
½ lb asparagus tips, cooked
1 pimento, cut in thin strips
salt
2 Tb wine vinegar
5 Tb oil
pepper

Remove outer leaves of artichokes, discard chokes, and cut hearts and tender inner leaves in wedges. Arrange artichoke wedges, potato slices, asparagus tips, and pimento strips on a platter. In a cup or small bowl, dissolve a pinch of salt in vinegar, add oil and pepper, then beat vigorously with a fork. Pour dressing over salad mixture, and serve either at room temperature or slightly chilled. (Egg Dressing or Creamy Mustard Dressing is also suitable for this salad; see Index.)

Asparagus Tips with Creamy Lemon Dressing

Yield: 4 servings

2 cups asparagus tips, cooked
1 celery heart, cut in thin strips
6 Tb oil
juice of 1 lemon
2–3 Tb heavy cream
salt
black pepper, freshly ground
1 small head lettuce (or leaf lettuce)
1 white truffle (or fresh mushrooms)

Put cooked asparagus tips and celery strips in a salad bowl. In a cup or small bowl, combine oil, lemon juice, heavy cream, and a pinch of salt and fresh ground pepper. Mix well, and taste for seasoning. Pour dressing over vegetables and toss to coat. Rinse and dry lettuce, and make a bed of leaves on four individual salad plates. Put a quarter of the salad on each plate, and garnish with paper-thin slices of white truffle (or fresh mushroom slices) to serve.

Asparagus Tips with Ham and Capers

Yield: 4 servings

about 3 lb asparagus
6 Tb oil
juice of 1 lemon
salt
black pepper, freshly ground
¼ lb cooked ham, julienne
1 Tb capers
1 Tb chopped fresh parsley

Peel, trim, and rinse asparagus; tie in bunches, and cook upright in lightly salted boiling water until crisp-tender, with tips just out of the water. Drain, rinse with cold water, then cut off stems up near the tips. (Stems can be saved and used later in soups and stews.) Cut asparagus tips in 1-inch lengths, and place in a salad bowl.

In a cup or small bowl, combine oil, lemon juice, salt, and fresh ground pepper, blending well; pour dressing over asparagus and toss gently. Garnish with ham strips, capers, and chopped parsley before serving.

Salad Royale (p. 65)

Aurora Salad

Yield: 4 servings

2 carrots
2 zucchini
2 stalks celery, sliced
¼ lb Swiss cheese, diced
1 small cooked beet, chopped
1 cup mayonnaise (see Index)
juice of ½ lemon
1 Tb grated horseradish
¼ cup milk (whole or skimmed)
salt
black pepper, freshly ground

Scrape and rinse carrots, scrub and trim zucchini, and blanch both vegetables. Drain while still rather firm, and cut in julienne strips. Combine carrot and zucchini strips, sliced celery, and diced cheese in a salad bowl.

In a cup or small bowl, mix chopped beet with ½ cup of mayonnaise and the lemon juice; then mix horseradish and milk, and add to beet mixture, blending well. Pour the dressing over salad mixture, and toss to coat. Season to taste with salt and fresh ground pepper, and top with remaining ½ cup of mayonnaise to serve.

Fresh Bean Salad

Yield: 4 servings

2 cups fresh white navy beans, shelled
4 slices bacon
10–12 black olives, pitted
2 hard-cooked eggs
juice of ½ lemon
½ cup oil
salt
black pepper, freshly ground

Cover beans well with cold water, and bring to a boil. Reduce heat, and simmer for about 30 minutes, or until just tender. Drain and let stand to cool. Fry bacon until crisp, drain on paper towels, then crumble and place in a salad bowl. Add cooked beans to the salad bowl.

Chop coarse 1 egg and the white of the other one, reserving the second yolk, and add to the salad bowl, together with olives. In a cup or small bowl, combine lemon juice, oil, and salt and fresh ground pepper to taste, mixing well. Pour dressing over salad mixture, and toss gently. Garnish with remaining egg yolk pressed through a sieve or food mill to serve.

Beet and Cauliflower Salad

Yield: 4 servings

1 small cauliflower, cooked
2 small beets, cooked and diced
4–6 radishes, sliced thin
1 small red onion, sliced thin
6 Tb oil
2 Tb wine vinegar
salt and pepper
1 Tb chopped basil

Separate cauliflower into flowerets, and place in a salad bowl with diced beets, radishes, and onion rings. In a cup or small bowl, combine oil, vinegar, and a pinch of salt and pepper, and blend well. Stir in chopped basil. Pour dressing over salad, toss gently, and chill lightly before serving.

Beet, Celery, and Ham Salad

Yield: 4 servings

1 head lettuce
1 cooked beet, diced
¼ lb boiled ham, julienne
1 celery heart, sliced thin
1 tsp Dijon mustard
1 Tb wine vinegar
salt
½ cup oil

Rinse and dry lettuce leaves thoroughly; tear in bite-size pieces into a salad bowl. Add diced beet, ham strips, and sliced celery heart.

In a cup or small bowl, blend mustard with vinegar and salt until smooth. Add oil, and stir well. Pour dressing over salad mixture, and toss gently to coat ingredients.

Beet and Onion Salad

Yield: 4 servings

1½ lb cooked beets
1 large sweet red onion, sliced thin
6 Tb oil
2 Tb cider vinegar
2–3 bay leaves, crushed fine
2 Tb chopped fresh parsley
1 tsp celery seed
salt and pepper

Peel and cut cold cooked beets in thick slices, then crosswise again in julienne strips. Put beet strips and onion slices in a salad bowl. In a cup, combine oil and vinegar; then add bay leaf, parsley, celery seed, and salt and pepper to taste, blending well. (Thin with additional oil and/or vinegar, as desired.) Pour dressing over vegetable mix, and toss gently to coat thoroughly.

Cauliflower Salad

Yield: 4 servings

1 medium-size cauliflower, cooked
8–10 anchovy fillets
1 sweet red pepper, julienne
2 hard-cooked eggs, quartered
salt
black pepper, freshly ground
2 Tb wine vinegar
6 Tb oil
3 Tb mayonnaise
1 tsp Dijon mustard

Separate cooked cauliflower into flowerets, and heap in a salad bowl. Garnish with anchovy fillets alternating with sweet pepper strips. Arrange a circle of egg wedges around the rim.

Prepare a salad dressing with a pinch of salt and fresh ground pepper, vinegar, and oil well blended and thickened with mayonnaise and mustard. Pour creamy dressing over salad mixture to serve.

Chicken Salad Amandine

Yield: 4 servings

1 cooked chicken breast
4 carrots, sliced paper-thin
¼ lb fresh mushrooms, sliced
½ cup blanched almonds
salt
juice of 1 lemon
½ cup oil
black pepper, freshly ground

Bone and dice chicken breast. Place in a salad bowl with sliced carrots and mushrooms.

Toast almonds in a preheated (350°) oven, or in a seasoned skillet, until golden; then chop coarse. In a cup or small bowl, dissolve a pinch of salt in lemon juice, add oil and a pinch of fresh ground pepper, and beat with a fork until well blended. Pour dressing over chicken and vegetables in the salad bowl, and toss to coat well. Garnish with chopped toasted almonds to serve.

Chicken Salad with Ham and Pineapple

Yield: 4 servings

½ cooked chicken breast
juice of 1 lemon
1 cup mayonnaise (see Index)
cumin powder
lettuce leaves
1 thick slice cooked ham, julienne
1 celery heart, sliced
2 slices pineapple, cut in chunks
1 Tb chopped chives

Bone the chicken, and cut in julienne strips. In a cup or small bowl, combine lemon juice, mayonnaise, and a dash of cumin powder, blending well.

Line a salad bowl with crisp lettuce leaves. In a mixing bowl, combine half the seasoned mayonnaise with chicken and ham strips, celery, pineapple, and chives. Fill lettuce shell with the mixture, and top with remaining mayonnaise to serve.

Chicken and Mushroom Salad with Curry Dressing

Yield: 4 servings

¾ lb cooked chicken
¼ lb fontina (or Swiss or other semisoft) cheese
salt
curry powder
2 Tb wine vinegar
6 Tb oil
black pepper, freshly ground
½ lb fresh mushrooms, sliced
2 firm ripe tomatoes, sliced thin
2 hard-cooked eggs, sliced (optional)

Cut chicken in wide strips, and dice the cheese. In a cup or small bowl, dissolve a pinch of salt and curry powder in vinegar; add oil, along with fresh ground pepper to taste. Place chicken, mushrooms, and cheese in a mixing bowl, pour dressing over mixture, and toss to coat well. Overlap tomato slices around rim of a glass salad bowl, spoon chicken salad into the center, and serve. (Salad may be garnished with egg slices and a sprinkling of chopped parsley or paprika.)

Frankfurter and Bean Salad (p. 57)

Country Salad

Yield: 4 servings

1 lb new potatoes
½ lb fresh green beans
salt
4 scallions
2 firm ripe tomatoes, sliced
1 cup cooked chick-peas
1 cup cooked kidney (or lima) beans
2 Tb wine vinegar
black pepper, freshly ground
½ cup oil
1 Tb chopped basil

Boil potatoes in their jackets. Cool slightly, then peel and slice. Trim green beans, cut in 1- to 2-inch lengths, and cook in lightly salted boiling water until crisp-tender. Trim green tops from scallions, and slice white stems in rings.

Arrange tomato slices, slightly overlapping, around the rim of a large serving platter. Distribute chick-peas, beans, potatoes, and green beans in separate mounds in the center.

In a cup or small bowl, dissolve a pinch of salt in vinegar, and add fresh ground pepper to taste. Gradually beat in oil with a fork, and pour dressing over salad combination. Sprinkle with chopped basil and scallion slices, and serve at room temperature.

Duck and Cheese Salad

Yield: 4 servings

1 medium-size onion
½ lb cooked duck meat
2 oranges
1 cup mayonnaise (see Index)
juice of 1 lemon
salt and pepper
½ lb Swiss cheese, diced
lettuce leaves
12–16 black olives, pitted

Slice onion, and separate slices into rings. Soak rings in cold water for 2 hours, then dry well. Carve duck meat from bones, discard skin, and dice meat. With a lemon zester or vegetable peeler, trim off the orange rind in thin strips. Next peel oranges thoroughly, removing white pith and membrane, and separate into segments. Bring a saucepan of water to a boil, blanch orange peel for a few minutes, then drain and dry.

In a cup or small bowl, combine mayonnaise, lemon juice, and salt and pepper to taste, blending till smooth. Pour dressing over duck meat, and mix to coat well. Stir in diced cheese and orange peel strips. Line a salad bowl with lettuce leaves, spoon in duck mixture, and garnish with orange segments, olives, and onion rings.

Festival Salad

Yield: 4 servings

2 firm ripe tomatoes, sliced
salt
1 head Romaine (or Boston) lettuce
1 lb small shrimp, cooked and shelled
2 Tb lemon juice
½ cup oil
1 Tb cumin seeds

Sprinkle tomato slices lightly with salt, and drain for 10 minutes. Rinse lettuce, dry thoroughly, and tear in bite-size pieces into a salad bowl. Cover lettuce with tomato slices and shrimp.

In a cup or small bowl, dissolve a pinch of salt in lemon juice, add oil and cumin seeds, and mix well. Pour dressing over salad just before serving.

Frankfurter and Bean Salad

Yield: 4 servings

1 hard-cooked egg yolk
1 small onion, chopped fine
1 tsp Dijon mustard
salt
black pepper, freshly ground
2 Tb wine vinegar
5 Tb oil
3 cups white navy (or lima) beans, cooked
6 frankfurters, cooked and chilled
1 small lettuce heart
1 Tb chopped fresh parsley

Mash egg yolk with a fork, and stir in chopped onion, mustard, and salt and fresh ground pepper to taste. Add vinegar and oil, and blend well. Put beans in a salad bowl. Pour half the dressing over the beans, and toss to coat.

Peel frankfurters, cut in 1-inch lengths, and arrange atop beans. Pour remaining dressing over the entire salad. Garnish with a few tender leaves of lettuce heart, and sprinkle with chopped parsley to serve.

Hearty Frankfurter and Potato Salad

Yield: 4 servings

2 medium-size potatoes
4 frankfurters, cooked
2 small onions
½ lb provolone cheese, diced
1 tsp oregano (or 1 Tb chopped fresh dill)
6 Tb oil
juice of ½ lemon
salt and pepper

Boil potatoes in their jackets, set briefly in cold water, peel, and dice when cool enough to handle. Peel frankfurters, and cut in bite-size pieces. Peel and cut onions in half lengthwise, then slice thin.

In a mixing bowl, combine diced potatoes and cheese, frankfurter segments, oregano, and half the onion. Combine oil with lemon juice, season to taste with salt and pepper, and pour dressing over salad. Toss gently, and garnish with remaining onion slices. Chill slightly before serving.

Gourmet Mixed Salad

Yield: 4 servings

½ lb fresh green beans
1 cooked chicken breast, julienne
¼ lb cooked ham, julienne
¼ lb Gruyère (or Swiss) cheese, julienne
1 small head radicchio (or chicory), shredded
1 sweet red or yellow pepper, sliced in thin rings
1 firm ripe tomato, cut in thin wedges
1 cucumber, sliced
2 Tb wine vinegar
½ tsp dry mustard
oregano
salt and pepper

Trim and blanch green beans in lightly salted boiling water. Drain while still quite firm, cut in 1½-inch lengths, and place in a salad bowl. Add julienne chicken, ham and cheese, shredded radicchio, and sliced pepper, tomato, and cucumber to the salad bowl.

In a cup or small bowl, combine oil, mustard, a generous pinch of oregano, and salt and pepper to taste, blending well. Pour dressing over salad mixture, and toss gently to coat ingredients thoroughly.

Green Beans with Peas and Ham

Yield: 4 servings

2 lb fresh green beans (or 2 10-oz pkg frozen),
  cooked
¼ lb fresh peas, shelled (or ½ 10-oz pkg frozen),
  cooked
½ cup oil
juice of ½ lemon
salt and pepper
oregano
¼ lb boiled ham, julienne
1 Tb chopped fresh parsley
2 hard-cooked eggs

Place cooked beans and peas in a salad bowl. In a cup or small bowl, combine oil, lemon juice, salt and pepper, and a generous pinch of oregano, blending well with a fork.

Pour dressing over vegetables, and toss gently. Arrange strips of ham on top, and sprinkle with parsley. Chop egg whites, and sprinkle on; pass egg yolks through a sieve or food mill directly on salad as a final garnish, and serve.

Green Salad with Cranberry Beans

Yield: 4 servings

3 cups cranberry (or pink) beans
salt
2 Tb chopped onion
black pepper, freshly ground
½ cup oil
2 Tb wine vinegar
1 small head lettuce (or escarole heart),
  chopped fine
1 Tb chopped fresh parsley

Soak beans overnight in cold water. Drain, put in a saucepan, and add water to cover. Bring to a boil, then reduce heat and simmer for about 1 hour. Season lightly with salt, and continue cooking until beans are tender. Drain and let stand to cool.

Place beans in a salad bowl; add chopped onion, salt and fresh ground pepper to taste, oil, and vinegar. Mix well, and let stand for about 2 hours.

Rinse and dry lettuce thoroughly, and stir in with beans. Toss gently to coat. Chill slightly, and garnish with chopped parsley when ready to serve.

Home-Style Vegetable Salad

Yield: 4 servings

¾ lb asparagus, cooked
½ lb cauliflower, cooked
½ lb fresh green beans, cooked
1 lettuce heart
1 head radicchio (or chicory)
4–6 radishes, sliced thin
8-12 black olives, pitted
1 Tb wine vinegar
1 cup mayonnaise (see Index)
salt and pepper
1 Tb chopped chervil and tarragon

Chill cooked asparagus, cauliflower, and green beans well; then combine in a large salad bowl. Shred lettuce and radicchio together, and add to cooked vegetables. Stir in sliced radishes, olives, vinegar, and mayonnaise; season to taste with salt and pepper, then toss gently to coat, and garnish with mixed herbs to serve.

Seafood Salad with Pickled Vegetables (p. 66)

Gourmet Shrimp Salad (p. 68)

Lentil Salad

Yield: 4 servings

1 cup lentils*
1 onion, cut in half
2 bay leaves
½ cup oil
2 Tb wine vinegar
salt and pepper
2 firm ripe tomatoes, cut in wedges
1 Tb chopped fresh parsley

Rinse and pick over lentils. Place in a large pot of lightly salted water to cover together with onion and bay leaves. Bring to a boil, then reduce heat and simmer for about 30 minutes, or until tender but not mushy. Drain lentils, and discard onion and bay leaves.

In a cup or small bowl, combine oil, vinegar, and salt and pepper to taste. Pour dressing over hot lentils, toss gently, and chill for several hours. To serve, place lentils in a deep serving platter, surround with tomato wedges, and sprinkle with chopped parsley.

Lobster Salad with Creamy Lemon Dressing

Yield: 4 servings

4 lobster tails (about 6–8 oz each)
vinegar
1 small celeriac (celery root), diced
1 endive, sliced
1 bunch radishes, trimmed and sliced
1 cup thick mayonnaise (see Index)
juice of ½ lemon
1 cup heavy cream, whipped
salt
black pepper, freshly ground

Split the undershell of each lobster tail with heavy kitchen shears, and put them in boiling water to cover, with 1 tablespoon of vinegar per quart of water. When water returns to a boil, cook for about 5 minutes, or until their shells become red. Remove the tails from heat, drain and allow to cool slightly, scoop out lobster meat, and dice. Place in a mixing bowl, and add celeriac, endive, and radishes. Chill thoroughly.

Blend mayonnaise and lemon juice in a large mixing bowl, and fold in whipped heavy cream until smooth. Pour half the creamy dressing over the salad mixture, season to taste with salt and fresh ground pepper, and toss gently to coat well. Spoon lobster mixture into a salad bowl, and top with remaining dressing just before serving.

Tangy Meat Salad

Yield: 4 servings

1 lb cooked beef (or veal)
1 Tb chopped basil
1 Tb chopped parsley
1 garlic clove, sliced paper-thin
1 Tb capers
2 anchovy fillets
salt
black pepper, freshly ground
2 Tb wine vinegar
6 Tb oil
1–2 medium-size red onions, sliced

Cut slightly cooled meat in bite-size pieces, and place in a salad bowl. Sprinkle with chopped basil and parsley, sliced garlic, and capers. Toss gently to blend, and let stand in a cool place for about 1 hour, stirring from time to time.

In a cup or small bowl, mash anchovies with a fork, and stir in vinegar. Mix well, add oil, and season to taste with salt and fresh ground black pepper. Pour dressing over salad, and toss to coat. Garnish generously with onion rings to serve.

Mixed Salad with Anchovy-Caper Dressing

Yield: 4 servings

½ lb small new carrots, cooked and sliced thin
½ lb shelled fresh peas (or ½ 10-oz pkg frozen), cooked*
¼ lb new potatoes, cooked and sliced
anchovy fillets
Tb capers
cup chopped fresh parsley
–3 Tb wine vinegar
½ cup oil
lack pepper, freshly ground
sweet yellow (or red) pepper, julienne
hard-cooked eggs, cut in wedges

Place cooked and cooled carrots, peas, and potatoes in a salad bowl. Chop anchovy fillets together with half the capers, and put in a small mixing bowl. Add parsley, vinegar, oil, and fresh ground pepper to taste, and beat vigorously with a fork. Pour dressing over salad, toss gently to coat well, and garnish with remaining capers and pepper strips, and egg wedges to serve.

*If frozen peas are used, follow cooking instructions on package, and cool well before using.

Salad Niçoise

Yield: 4 servings

new potatoes
Tb wine vinegar
lt
ack pepper, freshly ground
Tb oil
lb fresh green beans, blanched and diced
small head Boston lettuce
½-oz can chunk tuna, drained
firm ripe tomatoes, quartered
–8 anchovy fillets
2–16 black olives, pitted
Tb capers
Tb chopped fresh parsley

Boil potatoes in jackets, peel, let stand briefly to cool, and dice. Combine vinegar with salt and fresh ground pepper to taste, and beat with a fork. Stir in oil, and blend well. In separate bowls, toss diced potatoes and green beans with 2 tablespoons of dressing each.

Rinse lettuce, dry thoroughly, and make a bed of lettuce leaves on a platter. Arrange mounds of potatoes, green beans, and flaked tuna atop lettuce. Decorate with tomato wedges, anchovies, and olives. Sprinkle with capers, and pour remaining dressing over salad. Garnish with chopped parsley to serve.

Onion Salad

Yield: 4 servings

–12 small white onions, unpeeled
lt
0–12 black olives, pitted
thick slice spiced tongue, diced
Tb wine vinegar
Tb oil
lt
ack pepper, freshly ground

Simmer onions until just tender in lightly salted boiling water to cover, drain, and let stand to cool. Peel onions and place in a salad bowl. Add olives and diced tongue. In a cup or small bowl, combine vinegar, oil, and salt and fresh ground pepper to taste, blending thoroughly. Pour dressing over salad, and toss to coat well.

Italian Onion and Pepper Salad

Yield: 4 servings

2 large green or yellow sweet peppers
2 medium-sized red onions, parboiled
6 Tb olive oil
2 Tb wine vinegar
1 Tb prepared mustard
oregano
salt and pepper

Roast sweet peppers under the broiler, peel off charred skin, and cut in strips. Onions should be blanched, or parboiled very briefly, in order to retain firmness for slicing. Combine pepper strips and thin-sliced onions in a salad bowl. In a cup or small bowl, mix oil, vinegar, mustard, a pinch of oregano, and salt and pepper to taste. Blend thoroughly, and pour over vegetables; toss gently to coat well with dressing.

Peasant Salad

Yield: 4 servings

2 lb small new potatoes
½ lb lima beans, cooked
2 garlic cloves, minced
8–12 black olives, pitted and chopped
salt
2 Tb wine vinegar
black pepper, freshly ground
½ cup oil

Boil potatoes in jackets, peel, and place in a salad bowl, together with cooked beans. Sprinkle with garlic and chopped olives. In a cup or small bowl, dissolve a pinch of salt in vinegar, add fresh ground pepper to taste, and beat with a fork. Stir in oil, and blend thoroughly. Pour dressing over salad mixture, toss gently to coat, and chill slightly before serving.

Potato and Onion Salad with Marsala Dressing

Yield: 4 servings

2 medium-sized red onions, sliced
1 lb new potatoes
2 Tb chopped fresh parsley
⅓ cup dry white wine
⅓ cup dry Marsala
1 tsp celery seed
½ cup oil
salt and pepper
1 truffle (optional)

Separate onion slices into rings, chill in a bowl of cold water for 1 hour, then dry thoroughly. Meanwhile, boil potatoes in their jackets, cool slightly, peel, and slice. Place potatoes, onions, and chopped parsley in a large mixing bowl.

Combine white wine, Marsala, and celery seed. Pour over salad mixture, and allow liquid to be well absorbed, stirring occasionally with a wooden spoon. Drain marinated vegetables, and transfer to a salad bowl. Dress with oil and salt and pepper to taste. Grate truffle over the salad just before serving. (A tablespoonful or two of grated Parmesan or Romano cheese can be used as a substitute garnish.)

Shrimp and Mushroom Salad (p. 68)

Piquant Potato and Olive Salad

1 lb new potatoes
12–16 black olives, pitted
juice of ½ lemon
¼ lb Swiss cheese, diced
salt
½ cup oil
hot pepper flakes
black pepper, freshly ground

Yield: 4 servings

Boil potatoes in their jackets, cool briefly, then peel and slice. Cut each olive into 3 or 4 slices. Pour lemon juice over olives.

Place potatoes, cheese, and olives in a salad bowl, salt very lightly, and pour oil over them. Season with hot pepper flakes and some fresh ground pepper to taste, if desired, and serve.

Potato and Spicy Tongue Salad

Yield: 4 servings

2 new potatoes
Romaine or Boston lettuce (or leaf lettuce)
salt
2 Tb wine vinegar
1 stalk celery, julienne
4 sweet gherkins, sliced thin
½ lb spiced tongue, julienne
2 hard-cooked eggs, sliced
paprika (optional)

Boil potatoes in the jackets; drain while still a bit firm, peel, and dice. Rinse lettuce leaves, dry thoroughly, and line a salad bowl with them. Dissolve a pinch of salt in vinegar, add oil, and beat with a fork to blend well.

Combine potatoes, celery, gherkins, and tongue in a mixing bowl, and toss with oil and vinegar dressing. Pour salad into lettuce-lined bowl, top with egg slices, and chill until ready to serve. You may also garnish with paprika just before serving.

Princess Salad

Yield: 4 servings

1 lb cod fillets
¼ lb Swiss cheese, diced
1 sweet red pepper
1 cup mayonnaise (see Index)
juice of 1 lemon
¼ cup milk (whole or skimmed)
4 hard-cooked eggs, sliced
1 Tb capers

Place fish fillets in a saucepan, add water to cover, and bring to a boil. Immediately turn off heat, and leave fish in hot water for 10 minutes. Drain, cool, and cut in bite-size pieces. Place fish and diced cheese in a salad bowl.

Roast pepper by holding it on a long-handled fork directly over high heat on a gas or electric burner. Turn pepper frequently until the skin is blackened and blistered. Under cold running water, peel off charred skin. Slice lengthwise, remove seeds and membrane, and cut pepper in thin strips.

In a cup or small bowl, combine mayonnaise, lemon juice, and milk, and blend well. Pour dressing over ingredients in salad bowl, and toss gently. Garnish with egg slices, capers, and pepper strips. Chill lightly until ready to serve.

Salad Provençal

Yield: 4 servings

1 cucumber
salt
4 firm ripe tomatoes, sliced
4 anchovy fillets, chopped
2 smoked herring fillets, chopped
8 green olives, pitted
8 black olives, pitted
4 cooked potatoes, peeled and diced
½ cup oil
pepper
2 Tb wine vinegar
1 Tb Dijon mustard
1 medium-size onion, sliced thin

Peel and slice cucumber, sprinkle with salt, and set in a colander to drain. Arrange tomato slices on a serving platter. In a mixing bowl, combine cucumber slices, anchovies, herring, olives, and diced potatoes.

In a cup or small bowl, combine oil, salt, pepper, vinegar, and mustard, blending well. Pour dressing over ingredients in mixing bowl, and toss to coat. Spoon the mixture over tomato slices, garnish with onion rings, and chill slightly before serving.

Salad Royale

Yield: 4 servings

1 sweet red (or yellow) pepper
2 boiled artichokes
1 celery heart
2 cucumbers
1 small jar marinated mushrooms
2 hard-cooked eggs, cut in wedges
Lemon Dressing (see Index)

Roast pepper by holding it on a long-handled fork directly over high heat on a gas or electric burner. Turn pepper frequently until skin is blackened and blistered. Under cold running water, peel off charred skin. Slice lengthwise, remove seeds and membrane, and cut pepper in strips.

Remove outer leaves of artichokes, discard chokes, and cut hearts and tender inner leaves in wedges. Slice celery heart; peel cucumber, and cut in julienne strips. On a large platter, arrange separate mounds of peppers, artichokes, celery heart, cucumbers, and mushrooms. Surround with wedges of hard-cooked egg, and pour dressing over all salad ingredients.

Salad à la Russe

2 lb new potatoes
1 medium-size cooked beet, diced
1 cup mayonnaise (see Index)
juice of ½ lemon
1–2 Tb black caviar
salt

Boil potatoes in their jackets, drain, and peel. Let potatoes cool slightly, then dice and combine in a salad bowl with diced beet.

In a cup or small bowl, blend mayonnaise, lemon juice, and caviar gently and thoroughly with a wooden spoon. Pour the mixture over the diced vegetables, and add salt to taste, if necessary. (You may sprinkle with an added garnish of caviar to serve.)

Seafood Salad with Pickled Vegetables

Yield: 4 servings

1 doz clams, steamed and shelled
1 doz mussels, steamed and shelled
½ lb shrimp, cooked and shelled
½ lb baby squid (or other shellfish), cooked
1 pimento, chopped
2 new potatoes, boiled and diced
2 sweet gherkins, sliced thin
1 small jar marinated mushrooms, sliced
6–8 green olives, pitted and sliced
1 Tb capers
juice of 1 lemon
¼ cup milk (whole or skimmed)
½ cup mayonnaise
salt
black pepper, freshly ground
Boston lettuce
2 Tb chopped fresh parsley

Combine cooked seafood, pimento, potatoes, gherkins, mushrooms, olives, and capers. In a cup or small bowl, blend lemon juice, milk, mayonnaise, and salt and fresh ground pepper to taste. Pour dressing over seafood and vegetable mixture, add chopped parsley, and toss. Line 4 large scallop shells or small salad plates with lettuce leaves, and spoon out salad in equal portions onto the bed of lettuce.

Shellfish Salad Supreme

Yield: 4 servings

2–3 doz shellfish (clams, mussels)
½ lb small shrimp (or squid)
½ lb fresh mushrooms, sliced
8 Tb oil
salt
1 small head lettuce (or escarole heart), chopped
2 Tb lemon juice
3 Tb chopped fresh parsley
black pepper, freshly ground
2 hard-cooked eggs

Scrub and rinse shellfish well, and steam over high heat in a large, tightly covered pot with about 1 cup of water, until their shells open. Meanwhile place shrimp in a generous pot of cold water and bring to a quick boil, cooking for about 8 to 10 minutes in all. Drain and remove fish from shells, devein shrimp, then place in a large salad bowl. (Strain, cool, and reserve cooking liquids for other use.)

Sauté mushrooms in 4 tablespoons of oil, and season with a pinch of salt. Add mushrooms and chopped lettuce to the salad bowl. Toss with dressing made of 4 tablespoons of oil, lemon juice, a sprinkling of cooking liquid, chopped parsley, and salt and fresh ground pepper to taste. Grate eggs over the salad as a garnish when ready to serve.

Spinach and Bacon Salad

Yield: 4 servings

1 lb tender young spinach
½ cup oil
juice of 1 lemon
4–6 slices bacon, diced
salt
1 apple (preferably tart variety), diced

Clean and trim spinach according to directions given in the Introduction. Drain and dry thoroughly, then place in a salad bowl. Mix oil and lemon juice, pour over spinach, and toss to coat. Let stand for about 1 hour.

Sauté diced bacon until crisp. Drain on paper towels. Just before serving, season spinach lightly with salt, then add diced apple and sautéed bacon bits. Toss to mix well.

Shrimp and Mushroom Salad

Yield: 4 servings

½ lb fresh mushrooms
2 hard-cooked eggs
1 tsp Dijon mustard
salt and pepper
paprika
½ cup oil
juice of 1 lemon
4 Tb prepared chili sauce
1 tsp Worcestershire sauce
2 Tb dry sherry (optional)
2 Tb heavy cream
leaf lettuce
2 doz medium-size poached shrimp

Clean and trim mushrooms, and slice thin. Mash egg yolks in a mixing bowl, and add mustard, a pinch each of salt, pepper, and paprika, and blend well. Add oil slowly, while beating constantly with a fork and alternating with drops of lemon juice. Stir in chili sauce, Worcestershire, sherry, and heavy cream.

Line four small salad serving bowls with lettuce leaves, distribute mushroom slices and shrimp among them, and pour on dressing. Garnish with chopped egg whites to serve. (This salad may also be served as an appetizer in ice-packed shrimp cocktail cups.)

Gourmet Shrimp Salad

Yield: 4 servings

½ lb large fresh mushrooms
1 lb small shrimp, cooked
1 lb asparagus tips, cooked
4 artichoke hearts, sliced
2 firm ripe tomatoes, sliced
1 celery heart, julienne
1½ cups mayonnaise (see Index)
3 Tb oil
juice of ½ lemon
2 Tb tomato purée
1 tsp celery seed
hot pepper sauce
salt and pepper

Blanch mushrooms in boiling water for a few minutes, then cool and slice. Shell and devein cooked shrimp. On a large serving platter, arrange concentric circles of shrimp, asparagus tips, artichoke hearts, tomato slices, and mushrooms, with a mound of celery strips at the center.

In a small bowl, combine mayonnaise, oil, lemon juice, tomato purée, celery seed, a dash of hot pepper sauce (or Worcestershire), and salt and pepper to taste, blending thoroughly. Dribble ribbons of dressing over salad platter, and put remainder in a sauceboat for individual service at table.

Spicy Shrimp Salad

Yield: 4 servings

salt
1 bunch parsley
juice of ½ lemon
1 lb medium-size shrimp*
½ cup mayonnaise
¼ cup heavy cream
½ tsp hot pepper sauce
lettuce leaves
black pepper, freshly ground
2 hard-cooked eggs

Bring 1 quart of water to a boil, add salt, parsley, and lemon juice, then boil for 15 minutes. Add shrimp, and simmer for about 5 minutes, or until just pink. Drain, shell, and devein shrimp.

Combine mayonnaise, cream, and hot pepper sauce, blending thoroughly. Pour dressing over shrimp and mix well. Line a salad bowl with lettuce leaves, spoon in shrimp and dressing, season with a little fresh ground pepper, and press egg yolks through a sieve over the center of the salad. Slice egg whites, and overlap them in a circle around the garnish of egg yolk.

*If using frozen shrimp, cook according to directions on package, and add parsley and lemon juice to cooking water.

Stuffed Tomatoes à la Russe

4 firm ripe tomatoes
salt
Yield: 4 servings
1 new potato, cooked and diced
1 carrot, cooked and diced
¼ lb fresh green beans, cooked and diced
1 small beet, cooked and diced
2–3 Tb shelled fresh peas, cooked
¼ lb cooked ham, diced
1 Tb Dijon mustard
1 cup mayonnaise (see Index)
1 Tb chopped fresh parsley

Cut tops from tomatoes, and scoop out seeds and pulp. Salt tomato shells lightly, and invert to drain. In a mixing bowl, combine diced vegetables, peas, and ham. Add mustard to mayonnaise, and blend well. Pour dressing over vegetable and ham mixture, and toss to coat thoroughly. Fill tomato shells with salad, and garnish with chopped parsley to serve.

Tuna and Mixed Vegetable Salad

Yield: 4 servings

2 large sweet peppers
2 medium-size onions, scrubbed
2 medium-size zucchini
3½-oz can chunk tuna, drained
juice of ½ lemon
4 anchovy fillets, chopped
fresh basil leaves, shredded
1 tsp oregano
½ cup oil
salt and pepper

Cut peppers in half lengthwise, and remove seeds and membrane. Bake pepper halves and unpeeled onions in a preheated (350°) oven for about 20 minutes. Onion skins will slip off easily. Slice peppers and onions. Parboil zucchini for about 10 minutes; drain, trim ends, and slice thick. Flake tuna, and season with lemon juice.

In a mixing bowl, combine anchovies with cooked vegetables, then spoon into a deep serving dish. Sprinkle with shredded tuna and basil and the oregano. Season oil with salt and pepper to taste. Pour dressing over salad mixture, and toss to serve.

Windsor Salad

Yield: 4 servings

1 medium-size celeriac (celery root)
juice of ½ lemon
2 thick slices cooked tongue
3–4 sweet gherkins
12 mushroom caps, sliced thin
½ cup mayonnaise
juice of 1 lemon
1 cup heavy cream
salt and pepper

Trim and peel celeriac, soaking briefly in acidulated water; then cut celeriac, tongue, and gherkins in julienne strips. Combine these ingredients with sliced mushrooms in a salad bowl. In a small bowl, blend thoroughly mayonnaise, lemon juice, and heavy cream; season to taste with salt and pepper.

Pour half the dressing over the salad mixture, toss to coat well, and serve with remaining salad dressing in a sauceboat or small dish.

Zucchini with Mixed Herbs

Yield: 4 servings

1½ lb small zucchini, parboiled whole
salt
juice of ½ lemon
5–6 Tb oil
1 Tb chopped tarragon
1 Tb chopped basil
1 Tb chopped parsley

Drain partly cooked zucchini, trim ends, and—while still warm—cut in julienne strips or thin slices. Place zucchini in a deep dish and keep warm.

In a cup or small bowl, dissolve a pinch of salt in lemon juice; add oil and mixed chopped herbs, blending well. Pour herb dressing over zucchini, toss to coat well, and serve at room temperature.

Marinated Zucchini

Yield: 4 servings

1½ lb small zucchini, diced
2 cups dry white wine
½ cup oil
1 cup wine vinegar
5–6 parsley sprigs
2 garlic cloves, crushed
salt and pepper
sugar
1 Tb Dijon mustard
2 Tb chopped basil

Place zucchini in a saucepan. Add wine, oil, vinegar, parsley, garlic, and a generous pinch of salt, pepper, and sugar. Stir well, add cold water to cover, and bring to a boil. Reduce heat, and simmer very gently until zucchini are barely tender. Drain, reserving cooking liquid. Discard parsley and garlic, and transfer zucchini to a salad bowl. Cool cooking liquid, and combine 3 tablespoonfuls with mustard. Blend thoroughly, and pour the dressing over zucchini, sprinkle with chopped basil, and toss to mix well. Marinate for several hours, then chill slightly before serving.

Windsor Salad (p. 70)

Rice and Bean Salad (p. 72)

Chilled Rice Salads and Pasta Salads

Rice and Bean Salad

Yield: 4 to 6 servings

2 garlic cloves
1 small hot pepper (or hot pepper flakes)
2 slices white bread, with crusts trimmed
chicken or beef broth
6 Tb oil
2 Tb wine vinegar
salt
4 slices bacon, cut in thin strips
*3 cups cooled cooked rice**
1 cup cooked white beans
3 slices lean cooked ham, chopped
4–8 anchovy fillets
4–8 large green olives, pitted
1 tsp chopped fresh basil (or ⅓ tsp dried)
1 tsp chopped fresh marjoram (or ⅓ tsp dried)

Mash garlic in a mortar or small mixing bowl with fresh hot pepper (or a pinch of hot pepper flakes). Soak bread in enough broth to moisten, squeeze out liquid, and break bread into garlic and pepper mixture. Stir in oil, vinegar, and a pinch of salt, blending well.

Sauté bacon, drain, and place in a salad bowl with rice, beans, and ham; toss with salad dressing. Roll anchovy fillets around olives and garnish salad with them. Sprinkle with chopped basil and marjoram. Toss gently once more just before serving individually.

*Note: For all the recipes n this section, both rice and pasta should be cooked *al dente*, that is, slightly underdone and with a firm, chewy consistency. Also, all these salads may be served either at room temperature or else well chilled beforehand.

Chicken and Rice Salad

Yield: 4 to 6 servings

1 sweet red pepper
1 sweet green pepper
3 cups cooled cooked rice
2 cups cooked chicken, diced
1 Tb mustard
1 Tb chopped basil
6 Tb oil
2 Tb wine vinegar
salt and pepper
1 firm ripe tomato, sliced
2 hard-cooked eggs, sliced
1 Tb capers

Roast peppers on a long-handled fork directly over high heat on a gas or electric burner. Turn frequently until skin is blackened and blistered. Under cold running water, peel off charred skin. Slice peppers in half, remove seeds and membrane, and dice. Place peppers, rice, and chicken in a salad bowl.

In a cup or small bowl, combine mustard, basil, oil, vinegar, and a pinch of salt and pepper, blending well. Pour dressing over salad, and toss gently to coat. Garnish with tomato and egg slices, and sprinkle with capers to serve.

Cold Meat and Rice Salad

Yield: 4 to 6 servings

3 cups cooled cooked rice
½ lb cooked ham, sliced thick
4 thick slices mortadella (or bologna)
¼ lb fontina cheese, sliced thick
½ cup Lemon Dressing (or Mustard Dressing;
    see Index)
salt and pepper
8–10 stuffed olives

Place rice in a salad bowl. Dice ham, mortadella, and cheese, and combine with rice. Pour dressing over salad mixture, and toss gently to coat well. Season with salt and pepper if necessary, and garnish with olives to serve.

Peanut and Rice Salad

Yield: 4 to 6 servings

¼ lb Gruyère cheese
3 cups cooled cooked rice
½ cup unsalted peanuts, skinned
1 small white onion, sliced paper-thin
1 Tb chopped fresh parsley
2 firm ripe tomatoes, cut in wedges
½ cup Lemon Dressing (see Index)

Cut cheese in julienne strips, and place in a salad bowl. Combine with rice, peanuts, onion, and parsley, and stir well. Add tomato wedges. Pour dressing over salad, and toss gently to coat well.

Rice Salad Fantasy

Yield: 4 servings

½ cup raisins
pinch of powdered saffron
2–3 Tb milk (whole or skimmed)
1 cup mayonnaise (see Index)
juice of 1 lemon
3 cups cooled cooked rice
1 thick slice cooked ham, diced
¼ lb Swiss cheese, sliced thick and diced
¼ cup pine nuts (or unsalted cashews)

Soak raisins in warm water to cover. Dissolve saffron in milk, and combine with mayonnaise and lemon juice. Place rice in a salad bowl. Add drained raisins, saffron mayonnaise, diced ham and cheese, and nuts. Stir well to blend, and serve.

Rice Salad Medley

Yield: 4 servings

2 cups cooled cooked rice
3½-oz can chunk tuna in oil
1 cooked chicken breast, julienne
¼ lb cooked ham, julienne
¼ lb Gruyère cheese, diced
2 boiled frankfurters, skinned and sliced thin
2 firm ripe tomatoes, cut in wedges
1 large pimento (or sweet red pepper), julienne
3–4 sweet gherkins, chopped
⅔ cup oil
juice of 1 lemon
2 Tb chopped fresh basil (or 2 tsp dried oregano)
salt and pepper
2 hard-cooked eggs, sliced

Place cooled (or chilled) rice in a large mixing bowl. Flake tuna into the bowl with a fork, then mix in all other ingredients except the eggs and seasonings.

Combine oil with lemon juice, chopped basil, and salt and pepper to taste, blending thoroughly. Pour dressing over salad mixture, and toss well. Garnish with egg slices and a bit more chopped basil to serve.

Rice Salad with Mixed Vegetables

Yield: 4 to 6 servings

1 small eggplant
8 Tb oil
1 sweet yellow (or red) pepper
2 small zucchini, parboiled
2 firm ripe tomatoes, cut in wedges
1 cucumber, peeled and sliced
3 cups cooled cooked rice
1 cup cooked lima beans
juice of 1 lemon
salt and pepper
1 garlic clove
chopped fresh basil
oregano

Peel, dice, and sauté eggplant in 2 tablespoons of oil. Drain on paper towels. Roast pepper by holding on a long-handled fork directly over high heat on a gas or electric burner. Turn frequently until skin is blackened and blistered. Under cold running water, peel off charred skin. Slice pepper in half, remove seeds and membrane, and cut in strips. Cut zucchini in thin slices. Place eggplant, pepper, zucchini, tomatoes, and cucumber in a salad bowl. Add rice and lima beans, and mix gently.

Combine lemon juice, remaining 6 tablespoons of oil, salt and pepper to taste, and garlic, mashed in a press. Blend well, and pour over rice and vegetables. Sprinkle generously with chopped basil and oregano, and toss to coat well.

Rice Salad Medley (p. 74)

Spicy Shrimp and Rice Salad (p. 76)

Saffron Rice and Vegetable Ring

Yield: 4 to 6 servings

1 tsp saffron threads
1 tsp salt
1½ cups uncooked rice
½ cup oil
1 cup shelled fresh peas (or 10-oz pkg frozen), cooked
2 carrots, cooked and diced
¼ lb fresh mushrooms, sliced
8 sweet gherkins, sliced
black pepper, freshly ground
1 cup mayonnaise (see Index)
juice of 1 lemon
1 Tb Worcestershire sauce
fresh mint leaves
2 small zucchini, sliced thin

Dissolve saffron in 1 quart of water, and bring to a rolling boil. Add salt, and sprinkle in the rice. Cook over high heat, stirring occasionally, for about 15 minutes, or until rice is tender. Drain and cool. Place rice in a salad bowl, and combine with oil, peas, carrots, mushrooms, and gherkins. Mix well, and season to taste with salt and pepper. Spoon mixture into an 8-cup ring mold, rinsed in cold water and sprayed with vegetable oil, then chill for several hours.

In a cup or small bowl, combine mayonnaise, lemon juice, and Worcestershire sauce, blending well. Unmold chilled rice ring on a platter, and fill center with mayonnaise dressing. Garnish with mint leaves and zucchini slices to serve.

Spicy Shrimp and Rice Salad

Yield: 4 to 6 servings

1 small onion, chopped
2 Tb butter
1½ cups uncooked rice
2 cups chicken broth (or vegetable stock)
1 stalk celery, quartered
2–3 sprigs parsley
1 carrot, quartered
2 doz small shrimp
6 Tb oil
Worcestershire sauce
salt and pepper
¼ lb cooked ham, julienne
1 pimento, cut in strips
3–4 sweet gherkins, cut in spears
1 firm ripe tomato, cut in chunks
1 cup shelled fresh peas (or 10-oz pkg frozen), cooked

Sauté onion in butter until transparent. Add rice, and stir to coat grains well. Pour in broth, and bring to a boil. Reduce heat, cover, and simmer for about 20 minutes, or until rice has absorbed all the broth. Let stand to cool.

Meanwhile, make a bouquet garni of celery, parsley, and carrot and set in 1 quart of water. Bring to a boil, and cook for 15 minutes. Add shrimp, return water to a boil, then reduce heat and simmer for about 5 minutes, or until shrimp are pink. Drain and cool; remove shells and devein.

In a cup or small bowl, combine oil, Worcestershire sauce, and salt and pepper to taste, blending well. In a salad bowl, combine strips of ham and pimento, gherkins, and tomatoes with the cooked peas and shrimp. Pour dressing over salad mixture, and toss gently to coat. Add rice, and stir well to mix ingredients thoroughly. (Salad may be garnished with tomato slices and whole gherkins to serve.)

Sweet Pepper and Rice Salad with Lemon Dressing

Yield: 4 to 6 servings

1 sweet red pepper, cleaned and sliced thin
1 sweet yellow (or green) pepper, cleaned and sliced thin
1½ cups uncooked rice
1 cup fresh peas, shelled
8–10 black olives, pitted and chopped
½ cup heavy cream
juice of 2 lemons
salt
black pepper, freshly ground

Bake sweet peppers in preheated (350°) oven for about 10 minutes, or until just tender. Sprinkle rice into about 6 quarts of boiling water (water must remain at a boil). After about 5 minutes, add peas very gradually and continue boiling for about 10 minutes, or until rice and peas are just tender. Pour into a colander, cool under running water, and drain thoroughly.

Place rice and peas in a salad bowl, and add chopped olives. Blend heavy cream and lemon juice, pour over salad mixture, and toss gently to coat. Season to taste with salt and fresh ground pepper, and mix well. Garnish with pepper strips to serve.

Summertime Stuffed Tomatoes

Yield: 4 servings

8 medium-size tomatoes
salt
1½ cups cooled cooked rice
1 Tb chopped chives
½ lb Swiss cheese, shredded coarse
¾ cup mayonnaise (see Index)
2 Tb heavy cream

Cut tops off tomatoes, squeeze out seeds and pulp, salt shells lightly, and invert on a rack to drain. In a mixing bowl, place rice, chives, and most of the shredded cheese (reserving a few tablespoons for garnish). Combine mayonnaise and heavy cream, blend well, and pour dressing over rice mixture. Toss gently to blend, and fill tomato shells with salad mixture. Garnish with remaining shredded cheese to serve.

Tuna and Rice Salad with Beans

Yield: 4 to 6 servings

3½-oz can chunk tuna, drained
2½ cups cooled cooked rice
½ lb mozzarella, diced
2 cups cooked white beans
1 Tb chopped fresh basil (or 1 tsp oregano)
½ cup Lemon Dressing or Creamy Mustard Dressing (see Index)

Place tuna in a large bowl, and flake with a fork. Add rice, diced mozzarella, and beans. Stir briefly, and sprinkle with basil. Pour dressing over salad, toss gently to coat, and serve.

Macaroni Salad

Yield: 4 servings

1 lb small elbow macaroni
½ cup oil
3½-oz can chunk tuna, drained
peel of ½ orange
8–10 black olives, pitted and sliced
1 small jar marinated mushrooms, sliced
salt and pepper
1 Tb chopped fresh basil (or 1 tsp dried oregano)

Cook macaroni al dente, drain and cool under cold running water, and toss with oil in a salad bowl. Flake tuna with a fork. Slice orange peel in very thin strips; plunge orange strips into boiling water for 1 minute, then drain.

Combine tuna, blanched orange peel, olives, and mushrooms with macaroni; season to taste with salt and pepper, and toss to blend well. Garnish with chopped basil to serve.

Chilled Pasta Shells with Artichokes and Mushrooms

Yield: 4 servings

1 lb medium-size pasta shells
½ cup oil
4 oz marinated artichoke hearts, sliced
1 small jar marinated mushrooms, sliced
8–10 black olives, pitted and chopped
salt
black pepper, freshly ground
1 hard-cooked egg, chopped (optional)

Cook pasta shells al dente, drain and cool under cold running water, and toss with oil in a salad bowl. Add artichoke hearts, mushrooms, and olives, and toss to blend well. Season to taste with salt, if necessary, and fresh ground pepper. Salad can be garnished with chopped egg to serve, if desired.

Cold Spaghetti with Green Sauce

Yield: 4 servings

3 anchovy fillets
1 Tb capers
2–3 sweet gherkins
1 garlic clove
½ cup minced parsley
2 hard-cooked eggs, chopped
½ cup oil
2 Tb wine vinegar
salt and pepper
1 lb thin spaghetti (vermicelli)
1 small jar marinated mushrooms

Mince together anchovies, capers, gherkins, and garlic, and combine with chopped parsley and eggs in a mixing bowl. Stirring constantly, add oil in a thin stream, and then vinegar and salt and pepper to taste. Blend well, and refrigerate.

Break pasta in 2-inch pieces, and cook al dente in lightly salted water. Drain and cool quickly under cold running water. Put cold pasta in a salad bowl, toss with green sauce, and garnish with marinated mushrooms. Chill slightly before serving.

Index of Recipes by Category